Who's Afraid of a Large Black Man?

"A series of frank and probing discussions . . . with some of the biggest names in politics and pop culture—Samuel L. Jackson, Bill Clinton, and Tiger Woods among them."　　*—Chicago Tribune*

SAMUEL L. JACKSON ON THE WAY IT WAS: "For a while, if you were black, you were always the bad guy. Pick up a script and see what crime I did and which page I died on. That's what went on. The world was fine because we [could] kill them."

"The book's strength is directly proportionate to the force of [Barkley's] voice as an emerging leader of racial healing. While Barkley shows flashes of vaulted wit, he also reveals a deep concern for the cause of racial justice."　　*—The Washington Post*

CHARLES BARKLEY ON INJUSTICE: "When people talk about stars who have the ability to transcend race, what they really mean is, if you're a black guy, you've got to be the nicest guy in the world. You've got to be a nice guy all the time. Barry Bonds doesn't transcend race, for example. Even though he's the best baseball player of our time, he still isn't loved by white America."

"Charles Barkley may be the only figure in American life today with the finesse to slam-dunk a book titled *Who's Afraid of a Large Black Man?* in America's face and do so with a smile. Yes, he can be provocative . . . Barkley's barbs sting precisely because they have the ring of truth and address issues that his society would rather not face. [He] may be grinning, but inside he's dead serious as he goes one-on-one with thirteen guest stars on an issue that continues to divide the nation: racism."

—The News-Press (Southwest Florida)

ICE CUBE ON IMAGE: "I have a problem with black people who don't want to be themselves, because they feel it makes black people in general look bad in front of white people. White people don't care how they look in front of *us*."

"An engaging and surprisingly provocative book. Barkley used his celebrity to persuade other well-known people to sit down and talk to him about race in America. If you think there's nothing new to say on the subject, he'll prove you wrong. Barkley spoke to them individually, but their thoughts complement each other so well that the book seems like a discussion among friends. Barkley didn't have to write this book, but he did. When he says, 'I feel that [it's] the most important thing I've ever done,' you'll know what he means." —*The Arizona Republic*

BILL CLINTON ON HUMANITY: "My mother was a nurse, and she used to say, 'I don't see how anybody could be a racist who ever operated on people. Once you watch people bleed, it's all the same.' "

"A compelling collection of discussions between Barkley and prominent figures in politics, religion, and entertainment that provides a forum for a multitude of opinions. The goal is not to set the record straight, but rather to get a conversation about race started. And the book's straightforward, engaging tone is just right to achieve that end." —*The Charleston Post and Courier*

JESSE JACKSON ON MOVING FORWARD: "Free? We've gone from picking cotton balls to picking footballs."

> "Charles Barkley has never been afraid to express himself and no subject is taboo. When the former NBA great tackles the issue of racism, he does not tread lightly. His bold, straightforward approach in *Who's Afraid of a Large Black Man?* makes for a fast-paced, thought-provoking read."   —*The Tampa Tribune*

MORGAN FREEMAN GETS POLITICAL: "The only time I really got political was when we were trying to get rid of the Confederate flag in Mississippi. We still got it. You know what I'm going to do? I'm going to join the Klan. You can't beat 'em, join 'em."

> "When did Sir Charles *ever* need permission to be bodaciously outspoken? . . . In his new book, big Charles Barkley interviews celebrities about the big topic—race—and his outspokenness rubs off. . . . The provocative follow-up to his 2003 *New York Times* bestseller . . . *Who's Afraid of a Large Black Man?* is filled with . . . poignant tales, real-life vignettes about how people live race."   —*The Philadelphia Inquirer*

WHO'S AFRAID OF
A LARGE BLACK MAN?

CHARLES BARKLEY

EDITED AND WITH AN INTRODUCTION BY
MICHAEL WILBON

Riverhead Freestyle
New York

THE BERKLEY PUBLISHING GROUP
Published by the Penguin Group
Penguin Group (USA) Inc.
375 Hudson Street, New York, New York 10014, USA

Penguin Group (Canada), 90 Eglinton Avenue East, Suite 700, Toronto, Ontario M4P 2Y3, Canada (a
division of Pearson Penguin Canada Inc.) • Penguin Books Ltd., 80 Strand, London WC2R 0RL,
England • Penguin Group Ireland, 25 St. Stephen's Green, Dublin 2, Ireland (a division of Penguin
Books Ltd.) • Penguin Group (Australia), 250 Camberwell Road, Camberwell, Victoria 3124,
Australia (a division of Pearson Australia Group Pty. Ltd.) • Penguin Books India Pvt. Ltd., 11
Community Centre, Panchsheel Park, New Delhi—110 017, India • Penguin Group (NZ), cnr
Airborne and Rosedale Roads, Albany, Auckland 1310, New Zealand (a division of Pearson New
Zealand Ltd.) • Penguin Books (South Africa) (Pty.) Ltd., 24 Sturdee Avenue, Rosebank,
Johannesburg 2196, South Africa

Penguin Books Ltd. Registered Offices:
80 Strand, London WC2R ORL, England

The Penguin Press hardcover edition: March 2005
First Riverhead Freestyle trade paperback edition: February 2006
Riverhead Freestyle trade paperback ISBN: 1-59448-205-5

The Library of Congress has catalogued The Penguin Press hardcover edition as follows:

Barkley, Charles, 1963–
Who's afraid of a large black man? / Charles Barkley;
edited and with an introduction by Michael Wilbon.
ISBN 1-59420-042-4
p. cm.
1. Racism—United States.   2. Human skin color—Social aspects—United States.   3. Interviews—
United States. 4. Celebrities—United States—Attitudes.   5. Celebrities—United States—Interviews.
6. United States—Race relations.   7. United States—Social conditions—1980–.   I. Title.
E184.A1. B2444   2005
305.8'00973—dc22   2005043191

PRINTED IN THE UNITED STATES OF AMERICA

10   9   8   7   6   5   4   3   2   1

CONTENTS

ACKNOWLEDGMENTS

CHARLES BARKLEY:

I want to thank the wonderful people who spent some of their valuable time speaking to me for this book: President Bill Clinton, Justice Clarence Thomas, Tiger Woods, Senator Barack Obama, Ice Cube, Samuel L. Jackson, Marian Wright Edelman, Rabbi Steven Leder, Reverend Jesse Jackson, Marita Golden, Morgan Freeman, Peter Guber, George Lopez, Robert Johnson, Reverend Cecil Murray, Congresswoman Eleanor Holmes Norton, and Tom Burrell.

I would also like to thank all of my family and friends for their support and love. Thanks to my agents, Glenn Guthrie and Marc Perman, and to Lisa Hyman and Caroline Osterwise at IMG for their help, and to Michael Wilbon for another successful collaboration.

Most of all, I'd like to acknowledge the words and accomplishments of the black leaders of the past and present who created the opportunity for a book like this to be published.

MICHAEL WILBON:

My gratitude goes out to: Charles Barkley, for having the courage to take on this project and for bringing me along for the ride. My literary agent, Lynn Whittaker, for all of her help. Michele Clock and Jeanna Finamore, for hours and hours of transcribing all of the taped conversations. J. A. Adande, my friend and colleague from the *Los Angeles Times,* whom Charles and I pulled along for a chunk of the journey. Everybody at Penguin Press, particularly Scott Moyers, Janie Fleming, and Ann Godoff, for staying calm despite approaching (and missed) deadlines.

FOREWORD: HURRICANE KATRINA BLOWS THE ROOF OFF RACE AND CLASS IN AMERICA

I'm too young to remember what it felt like to sit at the dinner table and watch on TV as police sprayed people marching for freedom with water hoses and sent dogs to attack them. I'm too young to have seen it live on TV in the early and mid-1960s when police beat nonviolent protesters in the head and face with nightsticks. I've heard my mother and grandmother talk about what it was like to live through that, and I've seen the clips that appear briefly from time to time, but I can only imagine what the people who endured that—and who watched people endure that—must have felt like. I've always wanted to believe that that kind of mass humiliation was something we'd never see in this country again.

I know I never thought I'd see, in the United States of America, people begging for food and water for days on end. Think about it, even the poorest people in the country have regular access to food and water. But immediately after Katrina, they didn't. We're talking about the most basic necessities in the world—food and water—in the richest country in the world.

I guess I experienced the same feelings watching television that almost everybody else did. I was angry every day, and when I calmed down I was greatly disturbed. I still have certain images in my head of the people and the suffering they endured. I keep seeing this one lady, crying and begging for food and water for two days. I never thought I'd see people on rooftops all over New Orleans waving for help and writing messages, hoping somebody would see the message and save them. I never thought I'd see anything like that.

It's one of the hardest things I've ever seen in my life. And there's no escaping that most of these people were black, although there were plenty of white people, too. What almost all of them had in common was that they were poor. They couldn't afford to get out of the situation they were in even with a warning that all hell was about to break loose in the form of a Category 5 hurricane.

I watched it. I couldn't turn it off even though it was making me sick. After four days of being greatly disturbed, I couldn't take it anymore. I just couldn't sit. I didn't know what I could do at the time, so I flew to Atlanta and to Birmingham to visit shelters. I went to two in Atlanta and one in Birmingham. I had wanted to go to Louisiana, but I thought it was best to honor the wishes of the emergency workers who told everybody to stay away. I wasn't sure what I could even offer them other than to tell them I was thinking of them. It was depressing seeing total strangers sleeping side by side, day after day, on cots.

As I'm visiting the shelter at Georgia Tech, I hear people telling some of the evacuees that they had to leave. And I'm thinking, "Where the hell are they supposed to go?" And I heard the same thing when I was in Birmingham. The shelters needed the space for new people being brought in, and they were asking people to move on. How frightening do you think that had to be for the people who had nowhere to go, being asked to leave?

So I gave $250,000 in cash and I started the process to buy four houses in Atlanta for people to live in once they had to move. And even that didn't go exactly the way I wanted it to because of the red tape. I finally had the documents to sign the first few days of November, so that we could get people left homeless from Katrina into some housing. By the time people read this, I, hopefully, will have gotten a fifth house. And I wanted them to be in Atlanta. I'm sorry, but there's nothing happening for them in New Orleans and there won't be much happening there for them for months and months, probably years. My thought process was, "You've got to find people places to live." How long could they stay in shelters? To see mothers and fathers with two and three children in these places . . . It just tore me apart.

Some were white. A lot more were black. I don't know that anything in our culture in recent years demonstrated the divide between rich and poor like the aftermath of Hurricane Katrina. The people living in poverty we saw on TV didn't just get there—they're there all the time, every single day. . . . In so many of the conversations in this book, people acknowledge how much racism and bigotry has cost America, but people also talk about the economic divide being even greater than the racial divide.

Obviously, the journey via these conversations centers on race in

America and how it impacts everybody. But it's not possible to examine the impact of race without it being tied to the broader issue of
poverty and how this subset of poor white and poor black people are
so vulnerable and so linked . . . whether they know it or not.

When I was visiting people in the shelters it would hit me again and
again how much poverty, even more than race, had put them in this
position. It's hard for me to imagine, even now, how somebody could
lose everything he or she had in life. Yeah, some people with a little
money got caught up, but mostly we're talking about people who
didn't have much to begin with. It seems to me the great lesson that
has to be learned by the people hit the hardest is that if they can re-
cover from this and rally themselves, the next generation has to do
whatever possible to avoid being at the total mercy of anything,
whether or not it's a natural disaster.

I know that may sound a little tough, but look at how many people who were trapped didn't have a way out, didn't have transporta-
tion out of the Gulf region even though it had been evacuated for
days. Don't get me wrong, there's plenty of blame to go around. The
mayor of New Orleans and the governor screwed up, and the people
themselves screwed up by leaving themselves this vulnerable over so
many years to losing everything. That shouldn't happen. This kind
of helplessness in the face of an emergency just can't happen again.
That's the crippling part of poverty, being at the mercy of anything
and everything and having no means to fight back or at the very least
escape. . . . Get the hell out of that circumstance.

Hopelessness is the worst stain of poverty, and has been something I've always hated. That's probably why my first concern when I
was visiting the shelters was getting those children back in school.
That's the hope, that they can learn how to free themselves. It's not

going to happen through basketball or the entertainment industry, not for 99.99 percent of them. They're going to have to learn to do something to lift themselves out of poverty so that they don't have to live paycheck to paycheck. Hell, that kind of life can be wiped out by a whole lot less than a hurricane.

That's really what kept going through my mind when I visited the shelters more than who was to blame at what level of government. Believe me, I understand the anger and frustration people were experiencing. I understand Kanye West was angry and frustrated when he took a look at so many of those suffering people and said, "George Bush doesn't care about black people." But I didn't think that was the appropriate time to initiate that kind of discussion. You have to be really, really careful about accusing people of being racists and bigots. If he had said, "America doesn't care about its own poor people. . . ." now that's a lot easier to prove. In fact, there's no arguing that. There's plenty of proof. The aftermath of the hurricane, it seems to me, was proof of that. There were a lot of white people whose lives were destroyed in the Gulf region by that hurricane, and you can bet the people who fared the worst were the poorest.

Not only that, but the one thing we should have learned by now is that Americans rally, regardless of race, in the face of crisis. That's why it was so important for people who could afford to do something to actually do something. It wasn't easy. In both Atlanta and Birmingham I ran into people who had family members waiting to receive them and put them up indefinitely, but they didn't have the means to go. One woman had family in Sacramento waiting, two more had families in Dallas, another in New York. I would ask the Red Cross administrators on site why these people were still in a shelter when they were lucky enough to have someplace to go, and the Red Cross worker would tell me, "We can't just cut them a check or buy an airplane ticket. It just doesn't work that easily, unfortunately."

But it needed to work that way, at least for the people I could help. That's what a credit card is for. I couldn't help but think that without basketball, without the money I earned from being damn fortunate my whole adult life, that could have been me. I just got them to their families. I didn't know what to say to them. You just don't want to see anybody suffer like that, going days without knowing what's going to happen to them. A natural disaster is always a bad thing, whether it's an earthquake in Pakistan or a tornado in Indiana. But the aftermath of Katrina confirmed, unfortunately, many of the things I'd been thinking when I was having the discussions in this book. It confirms that as a country we don't care about *poor* people—black or white.

It used to be, you mentioned the city of New Orleans to most people and they'd immediately think about the French Quarter, Bourbon Street, Mardi Gras, the parties, things like the Sugar Bowl and the Super Bowl. That's the image of New Orleans most people had in their heads. But the tragedy in New Orleans has put something new in their heads. I bet most people didn't even know New Orleans is a predominantly black city. I bet they didn't know it's mostly a poor city. I bet they didn't know the poorest and blackest parts of the city were essentially a bowl that was just waiting to be filled with water and garbage.

That was all kept behind the giant curtain all these years, unless you visited the city and went somewhere other than the French Quarter. If you wandered away from all that, you could see some of the people who were there all along, people nobody noticed until the cameras showed them dying or begging or looting or rescuing people in canoes. It's such a sad chapter in American history, but such a great lesson in what we think about people because they're a certain color or because they don't have the means through education or income to move away from disaster. I'm glad I could help a few people, but when I start to think about those people begging for food and water, begging for their daughters and sisters not to be raped or harmed, it just makes me depressed all over again. And if we don't discuss what the hell happened down there in the Gulf at the end of August and through September and beyond, if we don't figure out what it is we should learn from the aftermath of Katrina, then we've let all those suffering people down again.

INTRODUCTION
BY MICHAEL WILBON

It was Mother's Day of 2002. Charles Barkley and I were just putting the finishing touches on his book *I May Be Wrong but I Doubt It*, which was Chuck's take on the world and the world of sports. He said—and I remember the words exactly—"I've got an idea for another book. . . . Tell me what you think of this . . ."

It was so clearly thought out, it was as if he had done an outline for this new book in his head. "Racism," he said, "is the biggest cancer of my lifetime. And I know I can't cure the cancer, but doesn't somebody have to attack it?" That simple idea was the inspiration for this book.

"I want to interview people who are influential in their various fields," he continued. "I want to talk to them about how race affects their lives and the industries they work in. It just seems to me people are afraid to talk about race. We're richer than ever, more educated than ever. The country is more diverse than ever. But I think we're more scared than we've ever been when it comes to talking about race. We spend more time and effort trying to cure racism than we spend trying to prevent it. Nobody wants to talk about what they think about people who are different until something really terrible happens, and once you reach that point nobody is rational. At that point, people are just stuck in their positions hating each other.

"I'm not expecting to find concrete answers," he said. "Maybe there aren't any to find anyway. I know people will disagree whenever race is a topic, but that's part of the point. We shouldn't be so scared to disagree or to argue that we just avoid something that everybody knows is so destructive. I want to try and start a dialogue. I want to sit down with people and have open, positive discussions about race and how they feel about where we're going, what's good, what's bad, what smart people ought to be thinking."

Charles stopped. "So what do you think about that as a concept for a book? And don't lie to me. If you think it sucks, tell me it sucks."

I loved his idea then and I've loved it even more since, as his editor, accompanying Charles along the journey he set out on. I loved it when we sat with U.S. senator Barack Obama one month before his election in Illinois and heard him talk about his vision for his state and the country. I loved it when we were having lunch with Samuel L. Jackson in Beverly Hills, hearing him talk about the times his paycheck was so small the bank teller smirked when he made the deposit. I loved sitting with Rabbi Steven Leder (who, as it turns out, I went to college with in the Midwest) in his office in Los Angeles, talking about what in the world has happened to a once strong rapport between Jews and blacks. I loved listening to *über*producer Peter Guber in his home on a Saturday morning talk about the forces necessary to break "tribalism" and how that affects Hollywood. I loved hearing Charles and Morgan Freeman, over dinner at Jezebel in New York City, argue like only two southerners could over the merits of NASCAR. I loved hearing Tiger Woods talk about why he will not compromise or reduce the fullness of his racial heritage for the convenience of those who can only deal with racial simplicity. I loved it when Ice Cube and George Lopez, both working on location, welcomed us into their trailers to talk about race and the entertainment industry. I loved it when Justice Clarence Thomas, even though he couldn't talk to us on the record because he has his own book coming out, welcomed us into his office in the Supreme Court and told Charles this book was an undertaking he had better complete. Justice Thomas told Charles not to let anyone trivialize his agenda, as he was on to something important, something worthy of serious discussion, and not to be afraid of disagreement, that you can't sharpen a knife without friction and that different and contradicting positions are necessary. He said that Charles has this platform, and he wished him all the success in the world with this endeavor. I loved it when Charles called excitedly from New York and said, "I just had lunch with President Bill Clinton in his office . . . you won't believe what he had to say."

People of great influence and sometimes fame picked up the phone or answered the door (sometimes only after great coaxing) because Charles was the one calling or knocking. And when they did, almost always they expressed to Charles that he would have better luck pursuing this particular dialogue on race, conversations that almost always begin awkwardly, than would politicians or religious leaders. Bill Clinton told him, "Charles, you are widely admired, because people think you speak your mind. If they don't agree with you, they at least think you told them what you think is the truth. And that's one thing you can do with this book."

It was clear that everybody who said "yes" to be interviewed had a sense of Charles's curiosity and his compassion. That was never more evident than in a discussion with Reverend Cecil "Chip" Murray, the senior pastor of First AME Church in Los Angeles for twenty-seven years. He had only one more month on the job when he welcomed us into his office one afternoon. His years of serving one of the most important churches in California included battling the L.A. riots, AIDS, police brutality, gang warfare, and hunger and facilitating the influx of a new wave of immigrants to Los Angeles, many of whom turned to his church for assistance. I had met Reverend Murray in May 1992, two weeks after the riots to be exact, when I was working on a series of pieces for the *Washington Post*. So I was happy Charles was meeting him before he stepped down. Murray has been a pivotal figure in Los Angeles, so respected that former governor Gray Davis came to First AME to share in that final Sunday. Reverend Murray told reporters, after his final sermon, "The black church must be a servant church or we are all in default. The church must reach beyond its walls. It must have more than prayer, more than worship. The word must become flesh."

So at seventy-five years old and having fought some of the culture's most destructive forces for all of his adult life, Reverend Murray was clearly delighted to see somebody with Charles's profile and influence wanting to engage people on the subject of race and the evils of racism. He looked Charles in the eye and said, "If this discussion comes from a Charles Barkley, it's got a chance. It's got a real chance to reach an audience that will take it in the right spirit. You're the right age, a young adult approaching early middle age. You've got the right background. You've had the right experiences. You've got a gifted mind, and you certainly have veracity. People believe you because they believe in you when they see your show on basketball every week deal with so many things beyond basketball. There are four guys sitting there exchanging ideas intelligently. But when they come to you, Charles, they know they're going to hear it straight. It's going to be truth, and it could be harsh. It's certainly going to be candid. You may not agree with it, but you will hear it. It's nice and clear and away we go. No shucking and jiving. If there is a person who can reach the multicultural community—men, women, young, old—it would be Charles Barkley. You can reach people in the political community because they're watching and listening to you. You're reaching people in the athletic community. You're reaching people of all races because sports is one of the few things in our society now that brings in everybody, regardless of race or religion."

While Charles is hardly unaware of his influence in certain areas of pop culture, he was undoubtedly taken aback somewhat that we were sitting in a church with a congregation somewhere north of fifteen thousand with one of the most prominent ministers in the nation's second largest city, seeming to suggest Charles should be leading these discussions. As a son of the South and a son and grandson of churchgoers, Charles is like a lot of forty-somethings in Black-World, who grew up identifying with national leaders, forces of nature who often were products of the civil rights movement, who at the very least got the attention of African Americans and often mainstream America on subjects as serious as race.

But Murray was quick to dispel that model as an answer. "Up to the sixties, we were locked in, looking for one door, concentrated on one leader helping us get it open, and there was a concentrated effort in that model," he said. "So here comes Martin Luther King, we somehow get the door open. And that door opens dozens of other doors. So now, instead of a single leader we have leaders on every front. We must have political leaders. We must have educational leaders, leaders in the world of medicine, leaders in the world of politics, leaders in community development, leaders in youth development. We no longer can work from the model of a single lone ranger to come riding in anymore. We've got to come at it from many different directions. What we probably need, rather than a single leader or leadership, is a single agenda. If we can agree on that agenda for the family, for the economy, for education, for the religious sector and so forth, then I think we could go into the twenty-first century. But we aren't going to get that one agenda, that one voice, because the NAACP right now has to reinvent itself. The Southern Christian Leadership Conference has to reinvent itself. And the church has to reinvent itself.

"One thing I've seen is the church, the religious assembly, has had to become a surrogate parent," Reverend Murray continued. "You have to become the father in most cases, or father and mother, for that child. Because many times the children don't follow the parent to church, or the children don't think church is cool. So the church has to reach out to the kids because the kids often don't have any parental connection to the church. We have some thirty-five youth components here and it really takes everything to keep those kids on board. Many of the parents themselves are not that involved. The grandparents are there and they don't make the kids come. So you have to make church extremely enticing or they won't be there. We have some five thousand kids, but you still have to really work at it because religion isn't a given. Showtime, Hollywood, media imaging is exciting to them. Some of it's positive, but so much of what excites them is negative, and you hear them calling women bitches and hoes and all these things they want to imitate. We have to find a way to offset all that negative imaging with positive imaging. What we've found is, if the church doesn't do it, it won't get done.

"Do you realize," Reverend Murray said, "that only thirty-nine percent of black children grow up with a mother and a father in the home? Just thirty-nine percent. That's compared to sixty-six percent of whites and Latinos and seventy-seven percent of Asians who grow up with both a mother and father in the home. So two out of three black children have a missing daddy, an overstressed mamma, and the kid is either raised by grandmamma or raised by the gang members. I think it will probably take from a half-century to a century to get the black family back to where it ought to be, and that's if we get some momentum and reverse some of these trends. Right now, we're at the point where the women, to a large extent, say, 'There are no men. I'll do without.' And the men who are there—these are our rare sons—they'll tell you the women come at them just because they're there, and that married or not married the women just pull at them. Just having so many black men in jail . . . so many more than are in college. We have a program for ex-felons, and we have 180 ex-felons in it. They come out of jail, we grab them right there before they go back into that web or that network on the street of drugs and all that stuff. And we work them through job relocation, home relocation, mentors. We hold them for about six months to a year, till they can see a whole positive light. But in the next two years, 465,000 brothers are going to be released from prison. That's almost a half million black men who are going to be released back to the streets with no skills. They can't vote. They've got one or two strikes. And if they pick up anything in the store, the three-strike law is going to eat them up. It's going to take a lot of time to restore that. It's not going to be a snap of the finger. . . . I know it sounds like I'm rambling all over the place, but these are some of the things you have to keep in mind when discussing race in America and why things are as they are to a great, great extent."

It's also important to keep in mind where the author is coming from. Charles Barkley was born in February of 1963, the height of the civil rights movement, seven months before hateful bigots bombed the 16th Street Baptist Church in Birmingham on a Sunday morning, killing Denise McNair, Cynthia Wesley, Carole Robertson, and Addie Mae Collins in one of the most infamous episodes in modern American history, one that a black Alabaman like Barkley can never let go of. He grew up in the projects. His grandmother worked at a meat-packing factory. His mother was a maid. Schools progressive enough to have both black and white students nonetheless elected one homecoming queen for the black students, another homecoming queen for the white students. Yet Charles's life was diverse because his mother and grandmother simply wouldn't allow him to exclude the way he had been excluded, and because he was a star athlete who was welcomed into places at Auburn University where another black student probably would not have been. He married a white northerner and together they produced a now lovely teenage daughter who asked her father, when someone inquired about her race, "Dad, am I black or white?" Her father's response was "Honey, that was determined for you a long, long time ago."

During one of our interviews—I think it was with Barack Obama—

the subject of interracial in-laws came up. Senator Obama is also the product of an interracial marriage. And Charles recounted a recent conversation with his own father-in-law. "He told me, 'I was a little worried when you married my daughter.' He said, 'I just didn't know at the time. But I've got three daughters, two of them married to white guys and one married to a black guy. And fifteen years later, the other two are divorced and you two are still married. I've already apologized for what I thought in the beginning.' It's funny, because obviously he went crazy when it first happened. But here it is, fifteen years later, and he says his daughter with the black husband and child is the one who's happiest in that context. It's interesting, perception and reality."

It's probably appropriate that someone with Charles's personal history with race be the one who sits and talks about it with anyone who will be open. Because he is who he is, he can ask anybody anything. And because he is who he is, people feel at ease talking about just about anything with him. Rabbi Steve Leder started our conversation by saying, "I think I can talk about the stuff with you I really don't talk with people about."

Charles could have written an entire book by spending a month exclusively with Reverend Murray and with Rabbi Leder. While one is Christian and the other Jewish, the men themselves seem to be coming from pretty much the same place. They confront and are affected by many of the same themes in Southern California, which because of its diversity can fairly thoroughly represent what is going on across urban America.

Rabbi Leder told Charles, "I'm so glad you're doing this, but I think your challenge is going to be to really figure out how hot the coals are. Maybe that's all that matters: that the leadership gets along,

and the grass roots doesn't matter 'cause it's hopeless or whatever.
Look, I just try to chip away at it every day. I try to do the right thing.
I try to be open. When you run a big synagogue—it's a twenty-six hundred family institution, ten thousand people—everybody with a worthy cause wants to come here to get the rich people in this
congregation to get behind it, or to help them with this or that. I say
no to almost everything because I'm very protective of the community. On the other hand, I say yes every time it's something like this—
starting a dialogue. But there aren't that many people asking to talk.
There aren't that many people who seem to care. I think that all communities have to push beyond the prior generation's definitions.
There's a saying that 'It's not incumbent upon you to finish the work,
but neither are you free to desist from it.' "

And that seems as good a place to start as any.

AUTHOR'S NOTE

Sometimes I think about how my life has turned out and I'm amazed. I'm thankful. I feel blessed to have traveled to the places I've traveled, to have earned the money I've earned, to have accomplished some of my professional goals, and to have met the people I've met. And because of all that, I feel I have an obligation to speak up and be involved if I see something I think is wrong or hurtful. I think others deserve to have the opportunities I've had in life, but in many cases people are denied those opportunities. I don't mean they're denied the chance to play professional sports. They're denied a chance to get a good education or have equal access to proper health care or jobs and promotions.

I've said a million times that racism is the biggest cancer of my lifetime. There's not a chance in the world I can eliminate it or solve it. But I can't sit around and say nothing. I can, because of my position in life, try to start a more public discussion of race and how prejudice just kills us all little by little. That's what I've set out to do here, to get people to discuss something that makes everybody uncomfortable.

I'm not an angry black man who's trying to lecture everybody. But I am in the unique position of being black and being somewhat famous and wealthy because of my career in basketball. If black people with some influence don't address this issue and get conversation started, then who will? Racism is a taboo topic, but it shouldn't be. It can't be if anything is going to change.

So that's why I'm writing this book. I was born at the right time in America. I came up in the South after Jim Crow laws were overturned. I came up at a time when the culture we live in encouraged people who were good at sports to perform . . . and be well paid to do it. But after enjoying all of those things this country has to offer, I can't just sit there, count my money, show up on television, and act like this ugly cancer isn't killing people in our society. Men like Martin Luther King Jr., Malcolm X, and Medgar Evers didn't dedicate their lives— and all those people, black and white, didn't march and picket and sit in at segregated lunch counters—just so people like me could have huge houses and fancy cars. So I've used my ability to get access to people I respect to discuss something I think needs to be attacked: racial prejudice.

I couldn't have done a book like this if I didn't trade on my celebrity. I wouldn't have been invited to speak at events like the Martin Luther King Jr. breakfast. I wouldn't be appearing on television every week. I enjoy those things and I'm having a wonderful life. But that doesn't mean I don't travel and see what hate and ignorance can do to all of us. And once I started these conversations it became apparent people of various races and persuasions had some of the same things on their minds that I did. And if you're not afraid to be a little uncomfortable at times, the following pages might wind up showing you that this is a conversation worth having.

WHO'S AFRAID OF A LARGE BLACK MAN?

LOOKING BACK AT THE BALCONY
TIGER WOODS

Since Muhammad Ali, probably no professional athlete has inspired more worldwide talk than Tiger Woods. That's because nobody in professional golf has ever looked like Tiger Woods. Sure, there have been people with dark skin who have had an impact on professional golf, from Charlie Sifford to Lee Elder to Jim Thorpe, all of whom are Americans of African descent, to Vijay Singh, who is Fijian. But Wood's ethnicity—his dad is African American and his mom is Thai—his dominance of the game at the turn of the twenty-first century, and his appeal to children touched off a golf revolution. Never had the game, invented in Europe and dominated by white men for four hundred years, grabbed the attention of so many blacks, Asians, women, children, and young adults as when Tiger Woods started a roll that would see him win all four major championships by his twenty-fifth year.

If Tiger Woods was a WASP and fourth-generation country club kid from New England, he would be a golf phenomenon. But as a black and Asian kid from Southern California who has been called "nigger" on numerous occasions as a child and as a teenager by people who didn't think he belonged on a golf course, he is a global phenomenon. People who operate under the impression that Tiger just sailed through life with no ugly confrontations will be shocked to learn that he suffered an ugly racial assault his very first day of school. But despite the odds, the "next Michael Jordan" from a marketing standpoint isn't another basketball player; it's Tiger Woods, who is probably the most recognizable athlete in the world, probably the richest, and in some ways the least known.

Anytime you look different from the others in your chosen field, people are going to be curious about you. And Tiger, quite obviously, looks different. He also *is* different. As a man who was born in the mid-1970s, he's not a child of the civil rights movement, as I am. He wasn't shaped by an America bent on segregation, as his father Earl most definitely was. But it's impossible to grow up in America with skin the color of Tiger's and not be affected by race. Because so many people, both black and Asian, see Tiger as representing their race, there has been something of a tug-of-war over him since he hit the PGA Tour in 1996, as much for the dignified way he behaves, dresses, and speaks as for his ability, which the golf community knew about by the time he was eight years old.

That tug-of-war has led to criticism of Tiger, that he should talk more about what race he feels he is, that he should identify with his African roots here in the United States, that he is wrong to shy away from issues of race, and the easy one that most people in public life face: that he hasn't done enough to help his race.

Having known Tiger since he came out of Stanford, I know that stuff is just a bunch of junk. I've told him dozens of times that he should talk about how he feels on the subject and damn the consequences. I've also teased him, when we talk about his multiracial background, that we know people see him as black because Thai people don't get as much hate mail as he does. Black people get that kind of volume of hate mail in America, not Thai people.

But the important thing for me was to hear Tiger talk about his own racial experiences, most of which he has not shared publicly until now. And with Tiger, you have to start at the beginning, with his parents.

"I was raised in two different cultures," he said one Sunday afternoon, sitting with me and Wilbon in Arizona. "I have my father, who is African American, and my mom, who is Asian, specifically Thai. I had to understand and appreciate more than just one way of looking at things because my dad's view a lot of times was the polar opposite of my mom's view because they were raised under two totally different cultural heritages. I was probably raised more in the Asian tradition because my father was working and my mom, who was at home more, was the disciplinarian. And a Far Eastern culture, as anyone who has experienced it knows, is very strict. So you have responsibilities. You had to do what you had to do if you were delegated a certain responsibility, and you never did anything to bring dishonor to your family. You can't disrespect anybody who's older than you, because if you do you've disgraced your entire family. That's kind of how I was raised, and from what I've seen it's a different philosophy from other cultures that I've been exposed to in America that are not Asian. If I didn't say 'Yes, sir,' 'Yes, ma'am,' 'Thank you, ma'am,' 'Thank you, sir,' I'd be smacked in a heartbeat, right on my butt. That's just how it was.

"Being raised under two different cultures gives my life a dichotomy that I think made me more well rounded earlier. And then there was the fact that I was playing a sport in which I didn't ever really play with peers. Golf traditionally is an older gentleman's sport. So as a kid I was always around people who had been in the workforce for twenty, thirty, forty years. There was a point in time—I was probably about thirteen, fourteen years old—when I told Dad, 'I'm more comfortable hanging out with you guys than I am with my peers.' But that's the environment I was raised in, so I was forced to grow up faster. You couldn't act petulant at a young age being around men who were very influential in what they did."

Everyone has tried to define what they think Tiger ought to consider himself. Because we all are asked at such an early age to disclose our "race" on applications ranging from driver's licenses to a form you fill out to give blood, people have to come to grips with choosing. I've told the story about my daughter asking me, "Dad, am I black or white?" and telling her that the answer was determined a long time ago in this country. Though her mom is white, her dad is black, so she's seen as black in America, and would have been three hundred years ago, when the child of a slave and slave owner was legally black. Hell, if that person married a white person and had a child, *their* child would have been legally black as well.

But this isn't three hundred years ago. There are so many kids of

so many races who cannot be easily described in a single box on an application. And Tiger Woods is one of those people who just will not be pushed into an overly simplistic description of who he is.

"I never tried to do it, or saw the need to because everyone else was trying to do it for me," Tiger said. "And it didn't really bother me. My whole objective was to try to win golf tournaments, and along the way I had my own challenges I had to deal with, being not the standard golfer. So I had to endure my own little bumps along the road to get to where I was. My dad went through it playing baseball. He was the first black to ever play in the Big Seven. It wasn't even the Big Eight yet. Now it's the Big Twelve. My dad played at Kansas State. He was the catcher. So my dad endured his hardships. He couldn't go to Norman and stay when the team played the University of Oklahoma. He had to go stay in Oklahoma City and then drive to Norman to meet the team to play, then find a black hotel. So his mom and dad always told him, if you're going to take advantage of opportunities you have to be twice as good to have half a chance. And that's kind of the philosophy that my dad raised me with.

"I was talking about this not too long ago with some kids. They asked me, 'What was it like growing up?' I said, 'It was great. But there were times when I wasn't allowed to play golf.' At the Navy golf course where I grew up playing, there's an age limit—at military golf courses it was ten and over. But for some reason all the white kids were allowed to play who were ten and under, though I wasn't. I had people who were older—and I don't know if they were servicemen or retired or active or guests . . . I don't know who they were—use the N word with me numerous times. I was there pitching, just pitching at a little chipping green. And they wanted to pitch, so they would yell at me and I'd have to go to the putting green. So I'd go to the putting green and I'd get yelled at over on the putting green. I'd go back to the chipping green, then get yelled at on the chipping green. These are things that obviously hardened me a little bit and made me realize that golf was not like basketball or football at the time. It was different, under different rules. Even traveling the country as a kid, I wasn't allowed to go to certain pro shops or certain clubhouses to change shoes where all the other kids were allowed to.

"Being black is just looked at differently. And in this country I'm looked at as being black. When I go to Thailand, I'm considered Thai. It's very interesting. And when I go to Japan, I'm considered Asian. I don't know why it is, but it just is. It shouldn't be about that but it is, unfortunately, because even as the world is becoming more global and more interconnected through all the different information streams, we're still very separate and distinct. People are trying to maintain their cultural heritage, even though we, in America, are probably the biggest melting pot of anyplace in the world. Now, being married to a Swede, it's interesting to see how excited she is when she's able to talk to a Swede. Or when my caddie Stevie, being from New Zealand, is able to talk to someone from New Zealand. I guess because I have more than one heritage I really don't feel that. The closest thing I have as a sense of that kind of connection is when I'm overseas and I run into someone who is speaking English."

But for Tiger, the sense that he was somehow different came very early.

"I became aware of my racial identity on my first day of school, on my first day of kindergarten. A group of sixth graders tied me to a tree, spray-painted the word 'nigger' on me, and threw rocks at me. That was my first day of school. And the teacher really didn't do much of anything. I used to live across the street from school and kind of down the way a little bit. The teacher said, 'Okay, just go home.' So I had to outrun all these kids going home, which I was able to do. It was certainly an eye-opening experience, you know, being five years old. We were the only minority family in all of Cypress, California.

"When my parents moved in, before I was born, they used to have these oranges come through the window all the time. And it could have not been racially initiated or it could have been. We don't know. But it was very interesting, though people don't necessarily know it, that I grew up in the 1980s and still had incidents. I had a racial incident even in the 1990s at my home course where I grew up, the Navy golf course. And right before the 1994 U.S. Amateur, I was eighteen years old, I was out practicing, just hitting pitch shots and some guy just yelled over the fence and used the N word numerous times at me. That's in 1994."

It's remarkable to me that Tiger has remained pretty much without bitterness. His life is nothing if not diverse. His wife is Swedish. His caddie is from New Zealand. His mom is Thai, and his dad is black and American. You don't see that every day, do you? Then again, maybe if we look closer, increasingly this is what we will be seeing as walls and barriers come down. Folks accustomed to being only with people who look like them may not want to see it, but it's there more and more if you just look around when you travel. Maybe part of it is

that so many people don't have the means or opportunity to leave their communities and don't know what's going on outside their segregated situations. Anyway, we know Tiger knows exactly who he is and has an appreciation for where he comes from because of some ugly lessons. Still, he seems not to carry that baggage around.

"My dad's mom died when he was about thirteen years old, but he said her philosophy, which he's always followed, was: Always give everyone a chance. Always. And it doesn't matter what race the person is, what their economic background is. None of it matters. Just talk to them. Don't presume you know what a person is thinking or feeling. Just talk to them and find out for yourself.

"Over time, my attitude has changed about this issue. When I was little, it was about trying to help people who were black. As I've grown older I've come to the decision that I don't want to take that particular approach anymore. I want to help everybody. So my foundation will be done with that in mind. It's the Start Something program, a mentoring program. I don't care who you are, what race you are, or what your ethnicity is. Don't ask me to care. It's about helping the next generation have a better future. And I will be a leader for everybody. Not just one group. I don't want to limit myself, and I won't be pigeonholed. I just feel like I can do more than be a leader strictly to blacks or strictly to Asians. I want to be a leader to everybody and that means globally. That means taking my foundation and going around the world and doing something to help anybody. I'm not going to limit myself to just one race, one religion, or one sex. Any effort I'm involved with is going to be about everybody.

"People want to pigeonhole me or move me in a certain direction that speaks to their agenda. And I've obviously been distanced in my takes in certain political situations because I don't want to be pushed in their direction or be forced to take a particular view. I have my own views. I'm trying to do my best right now with what I have, growing my foundation and using it to be a springboard to the future. We have three million kids right now in the Start Something program. We're trying to work within the next year and a half to go global with it.

"Another of the things that I've realized from traveling around the world and playing all over the place is: The only way to make a difference is to be informed. You have to be informed. You have to have knowledge. You have to have an education. You have to realize how important it is to be able to read and write, develop your mind, to be able to articulate your ideas and communicate with anyone.

"I'm not going to play golf forever. When I think I'm not good enough to play anymore and win, I'm gone. I've always told my friends that, and they all think I'm crazy. My dad laughs at me sometimes when I say that when I do quit, when I'm done, I don't need to be remembered as a golfer. I want to be remembered for whatever social impact I've had around the world. Some people remember Arthur Ashe because he was a tennis player. But there are people all around the world who don't know that he won Wimbledon but remember what kind of social impact he made, what kind of leader he was. That's the kind of role I want to play and be remembered for playing. 'Yeah,' people might say, 'he was a good golfer at one point. You know, he won some tournaments here and there. But what he did socially had a real impact.' "

When you're a professional athlete, you don't always see what's going on around you because you have to have tunnel vision to com-

pete with the best in the world at what you do. So I've wondered if Tiger knows how many black people play golf because of him, how the galleries have changed since he joined the tour, how much more inclusive the industry of golf has had to become. He forced all of that. The people who ran and enjoyed golf and had it as their own and kept it to themselves weren't trying to run out and share it with everybody. In Europe and around the world, golf is a working-class game. But in America, it's been pretty much the same country club sport for a hundred years. It's radically different now. And as much as men like Charlie Sifford and Lee Elder and Lee Trevino and others broke down the first barriers of racism, the whole thing didn't change radically until Tiger. I know I had never been to a college golf tournament until somebody told me, "Tiger Woods is in town." And I said, "I'd like to see that." And I went. But really, I had never watched golf in my life before. Now, I build my weekend around what time Tiger's coming on TV. So I asked him if he's aware of the impact he's already had.

"When you're in the hole it's really hard to see out of it," Tiger said. "You can be so close to something that you're not aware of all that's around. Your view is very one-dimensional. I don't get the chance to see all of that. But what I have seen is that when I go to tournaments now, the galleries are much more diverse. We're talking about more women. We're talking about more minorities. Plus just a boatload of kids, which is very exciting to see. To see these kids just smiling away and thinking it's just so cool to be out there watching golf. When I was growing up, it wasn't a cool thing. Even when I was in high school, you were considered a wuss for playing golf. It wasn't a cool thing to do. Everybody played basketball, football, baseball, or ran track—the core sports in America. If you're back East, maybe you play hockey or lacrosse, but I was in L.A. There wasn't even a thought to play golf for most people. That wasn't a cool sport to play at all. But now, to see other kids playing golf, to hear them say 'I'm not going to play football or basketball or run track or baseball; I'm going to play golf' is just very different."

Same thing with tennis. Look at what the Williams sisters are doing. I mean, that brought a whole new burst to that sport.

"I think people should have the opportunity to play whatever sport they choose, whatever sport they want to play," Tiger said. "They shouldn't be denied an opportunity to participate or be discouraged by anyone to participate, whether the sport is popular with a certain group of people or not. That shouldn't ever happen. Not ever. I try to preach that at all of my speaking engagements around the country, and overseas for that matter. We're not providing enough, given our opportunity. We're not doing our job. I'm trying to do more with the vehicle that I have, which is through golf and through my foundation, and mentoring and role modeling. That's one area where I feel like I have an understanding—not a complete understanding, but at least enough of an understanding to be able to help. I think the Tour embraces it from a marketing standpoint. The Tour is about business. What I'm trying to do is run a humanitarian foundation. There are two different ways to look at it: I'm trying to give money away; the Tour is trying to make money. So you can't really compare the two efforts."

Funny thing is that even with Tiger's success and impact and the increased number of kids joining minority golf programs and programs like First Tee, we haven't seen any real change in the number of African Americans playing on any of the tours, or African Asians for that matter . . . not on the men's tour anyway.

"I would make the case," Tiger said, "that it's still a numbers issue. Even when we had Calvin Peete, Jim Thorpe, Charlie Sifford, and Lee Elder out there on tour, we had a very small base to work from. If we can grow the base, you're going to pyramid up and you'll have a few more make it to the Tour. As I travel the country and do clinics I see these kids with technically sound golf swings at ten, twelve years old who are black. I never saw that when I first started playing the Tour. Technology has certainly helped, because now they can videotape and analyze their swings and become better. Now it's a cool sport to play, and professional athletes are playing, which even adds to that coolness. To have you playing, Charles, Michael Jordan playing, that brings a whole new excitement level to a sport that people thought was just a game for WASPs. But now you have some of the most powerful athletes in the world playing golf? 'Hey,' kids say, 'we should take a look at this; we never thought that was an option.'

"Obviously, I had some success, and that has something to do with it. I came along and got lucky with the timing. Just as Arnold Palmer had the right timing because he came along at the same time television was exploding in America. Now, we've got global Internet access. Our sport wasn't global when I began playing the Tour. Now it is. You can log on anywhere in the world and see what any player did in any tournament or for the year. You can follow the PGA or the European

Tour. With that international boom, that international stream of information, golf is getting exposed to parts of the world that it never even thought of getting into. That's all about timing."

Okay, that's nice. But even if the time is right, the person has to come along, and he or she has to be willing to use the leverage they have at that time to make change.

"You know, we've had to use that," Tiger said. "I don't like using it, but we've had to use it in order to get the funds to be able to do what we do. That's why Target has been so influential with us. That's why it's the Target Start Something program. We started working with Target in 1999, at St. Jude's Hospital, with what they do with cancer patients. We built a library for them. Although I don't like using that kind of personal leverage, sometimes you really have to in order to get the funds to be able to do what you want to do.

"But it's also a matter of getting in there face to face and explaining to people what we're trying to do. For that, it's a matter of education and articulation. It's essential to be able to articulate your points. You can't just say, 'Hey, gimme your money, I'm going to try to help kids.' You can't do that. It's a lot more detailed than that. You have to be able to articulate your opinion, you really do.

"That's why I try to emphasize with kids how important education is. I dropped out of school and turned pro in 1996 when I still had two more years of Stanford. But does that mean my education stopped there? No, it's just starting. Now I'm in a whole new world, but I still read a boatload. I still watch TLC, the Discovery Channel, all these learning shows, because I like learning. I enjoy learning.

Just because I dropped out of school doesn't mean I ever quit learning. Maybe I'm not going to school now, but I can gain knowledge anywhere and everywhere."

You cannot talk about Tiger Woods and race without dealing with his win at Augusta National in 1997, a historic win not just because Tiger was the first person of color to win there—a place that even now, because of its stance on women not being members, symbolizes exclusion and golf's lingering intolerance—but because he won by a record margin. Many black people in America didn't even know what the Masters Tournament was before that weekend. They certainly had never watched. I don't know if any studies have been done, but my bet is that there were millions of Asians and Hispanics around the world who had never watched golf before, but watched the Masters on that Sunday afternoon when Tiger won.

There's a memory from that day that has nothing to do with golf that Tiger shared during our conversation that afternoon. His tone turned very serious as he recalled it. After the traditional ceremony at Butler Cabin to present him with the customary green jacket, Tiger had something else waiting for him, something that was very rewarding in a different sense.

"So, there's this closing ceremony," Tiger explained. "You go on the putting green, where it takes place, and I look up and they're all there in their white outfits. The cooks, the staff, attendants, everybody. They're all black. Each one of them came out onto the balcony and watched it. I look back and I start getting choked up just thinking about it. They touched me in a really powerful way. I started thinking about everything these people had faced in life, all the ugliness and all the prejudice and all the obstacles they had to deal with. I've seen what they struggle with and I feel so bad. I was thinking that they could have a lot of bitterness and feel 'Why him? Why not me?' But they didn't. They don't. It was very impactful, man. It was so huge to me, for them to feel that way about me and for them to honor me in that way.

"I've gotten to know most of those people now, learning about all the years they worked there. And it's really that I want to say thank you to them because they influenced my life. They touched me more than they will ever know. Ever. As I walked out that day, I said, 'Dad, look up there in the clubhouse. Just look over there.' And my dad started getting choked up. 'Son,' he said, 'take this in.' And I said, 'Dad, that's what I've been doing. I've been looking over there the entire time.' "

POLITICAL RACE/S
BARACK OBAMA

Even people who are very aware politically might not have heard the name Barack Obama until sometime in the spring or summer of 2004. Even people in Illinois didn't know who he was two years ago. It was that great emotional speech, at the 2004 Democratic National Convention, that was a combination of intelligence and Sunday morning at the pulpit that got people really familiar with him. Now he's a U.S. senator, and only the third person of color to hold that position since Reconstruction.

The phrase "African American" really doesn't tell you anything specific about a person's background other than that he or she has some African ancestry, and that he or she is an American citizen. We as black people always laugh about it because we know how mixed-race 90 percent of us are. The label "African American" doesn't tell you, for instance, that a whole lot of black people have at least one Native American grandparent or great-grandparent.

Barack Obama is the son of a father who is African and a mother who is white and from Kansas. How many elected officials in America have a profile similar to that? He's kind of like the changing face of the country. He's hard to peg, which makes it interesting because his background means he sees the world from a perspective that's probably different from everybody else's. I think people don't know what exactly to make of him, and how who he is racially impacts what he believes socially and politically.

He has a chance to be a great leader for black people, for a lot of people for that matter. When you see him and hear him speak, you can tell how smart he is. Plus, he has great charisma. For a long time, the guy who did most of the speaking for black people was Jesse Jackson. I'm not sure kids today still identify with Jesse as he gets older. They need somebody to follow. Barack has that type of charisma— kind of like Bill Clinton.

One of the keys for a black leader to be effective is that white people can't be afraid of him. White people have all the money and power, and if they're going to help black people, if they're going to listen to their complaints, they have to be approached in a nonthreatening way. Barack puts everybody at ease.

When Wilbon and I went to his offices on South Michigan Avenue in Chicago, it was just before the November 2004 election. His opponent was Alan Keyes, the ultra-conservative commentator whom white Republicans had picked to run against Barack after Jack Ryan, the person they really wanted to run, had to withdraw from the race because of a sex scandal that involved his wife but didn't actually have

sex in it. . . . But that's another story. Barack seemed like a real transitional politician in America and ever since I heard about him, how
he graduated from Harvard Law, where he met his wife, I wanted to
know about his life and his plans and how his background affects his
plans and how he is perceived.

He had gone to a place called Cairo, Illinois, down in the southern part of the state, to campaign. It's a part of the state that is conservative, definitely one of the least liberal parts of Illinois, way away
from Chicago and the center of black urban politics. But he was able
to connect with the rural, overwhelmingly white population there in
a way no black politician ever had . . . the way no black politician had
ever dreamed of trying. I must admit it's rather shocking, so I wanted
to know how in the hell he did it and what it might mean. Maybe he's
the one person who in four or eight or twelve years can help heal a
nation that is divided politically, socially, religiously, and most of all
racially.

Barack told us that when he had his eye on a seat in the Senate,
"The general view was 'He'd be a great U.S. senator, but he is not
gonna be able to get in.' The attitude was 'He's got no money, he
doesn't come from a wealthy family, he's got no organization, he wasn't
born into a political family, and he's a black man with this name that
folks can't even pronounce. And it sounds Muslim! So, he's not gonna
be able to get through the difficulties of the campaign process.'

"But my general attitude was obviously much more optimistic than
that because I had seen how people responded if I met them one-on-
one or if I met them in a group. My attitude has always been if you
put me in a room with anybody, I don't care whether the people are

white, black, Asian, Hispanic. If you put me in a room with them and just give me half an hour to talk to them, then I'll be able to find some sort of connection with them. And they'll respond, 'Okay, here's a guy who's sincere and knows what he is talking about.' "

But even if people feel that way on a grassroots level, there's still the issue of getting the message out.

"There were basically two components," Barack said. "One was being able to raise enough money. Would we be able to do TV advertising, because there is nothing more powerful than TV. The second thing was just barnstorming around the state and attracting diverse crowds. It was a matter of slowly building them, getting more and more people to start coming out and having a conversation with them. And it worked.

"I think part of it goes to the question you are dealing with in this book: about race. There is no doubt that race is a continuing and enormous factor in American life. Always has been. It's sort of the fundamental stain on American life. But what is also true is usually American people are more decent than I think a lot of folks give them credit for. Even when conflicts arise, you sometimes get the sense that they're busy, they're tired, they're stressed about whatever issues are affecting them, and a lot of times, they will just make assumptions about other groups because they haven't been exposed to them. But if you can talk to them in terms of common values and things that they share, if you talk about kids, jobs, health care and things everybody has an aspiration toward, then I think people will respond. And that's what happened in the case of our campaign. We were sort of an underdog. It's like sports: If you're Seabiscuit, if you're the one who on paper folks don't think is gonna win and then wins, it is that much bigger.

"That win put us on the map. After I won the primary, people stood back and said 'How did this happen?' particularly because we won the white voters. The state had one guy who spent thirty million dollars, another guy who was the city and state comptroller and had endorsements from all the Democratic organizations around the state. And we beat them by thirty points. I mean, we won the white voters. It wasn't just like we barely won. Our theory was that we would do well, and in a seven-person primary race we thought we'd get about 25 percent of the white vote. But then we ended getting 90 percent of the black voters, and then for us to get more than 25 percent, yes, it surprised us."

But why should it be a surprise? Why should he have been the underdog? Now here's a guy who graduated magna cum laude from Harvard Law School and became the first black president of the Harvard Law Review. He taught law at the University of Chicago. He served in the Illinois State Senate. He's brilliant and successful. And he still started in the last row. Why do you think that is? Is race that much of an impediment?

Arnold Schwarzenegger sat in the driver's seat in the governor's race in California, even though his claims to fame were that he lifted weights and played an indestructible robot in the movies. He wasn't even born in America. Now there's talk about a constitutional amendment so the Austrian-born Schwarzenegger can be elected president. Do you realize how hard it is to amend the constitution? It's only hap-

pened twenty-seven times in the history of our country. And they want to make it twenty-eight just because of Arnold Schwarzenegger?

They're trying to change the rules in Schwarzenegger's favor, but Barack needed to get lucky to beat the field. His top two competitors were taken out by sex scandals or else no one would be talking about him today. Here's a guy who's so qualified, it's scary, but still everything had to break perfectly for him.

Now they're saying, "Oh, he's brilliant. He's charismatic." But why did it take all of that other junk for him to get here? That's what's frustrating to me.

Barack's political story has just started, relatively speaking. At least, the campaigning and running for public office just started. But who he is, what he believes in, and how he sees himself in the context of being a person of color in America and how important that is were formed awhile ago. One of the things I'm curious about is when does a person with one black parent and one white parent become aware of race. Barack uses the term *unusual* to describe his background, and not just because he is biracial, but because of how and where he grew up.

"I was born in Hawaii," he said. "My father was from Kenya, my mother is a white woman from Kansas. In my early years, I lived in Hawaii where just about everybody is mixed up racially, for better or for worse. I really didn't think about race in those terms the first six years of my life. Then I moved to Indonesia, because my mother was involved in international development and she remarried after she and my father divorced. So I lived in Asia and there are people who noticed I was different. First of all, I'm taller than everybody else.

Everybody else was probably about five feet tall. So they all thought I was fifteen, when I'm, you know, six. I'm serious, the average height for men was like five-three or something. . . . Anyway, I remember being in the American embassy in Jakarta and, in fact, the head of the embassy there was a black guy. He was a very distinguished and very impressive guy.

"My mother worked in the embassy, so she would sometimes let me go to the library there and I would start looking through books, read comic books. But then I'd read some other stuff. I remember getting this *Life* magazine and flipping through the pages. And I came across this picture of this white guy, but something about him looks kinda funny. He looks real . . . pale, he looks like he's an albino or something. There was something not quite right about him. I couldn't figure it out at first, so I start reading the piece and it turns out it wasn't a white guy, it was a black guy who had bleached his skin with these skin-lightening products that used to be around in the 1950s. The story was about all these black folks who had gone through this bleaching process and the results were terrible. I mean they looked just awful, and they talked in the interview about how sorry they were about having gone through all they went through, psychologically, and then, of course, the physical act of trying to bleach themselves.

"I remember that was the first time when I thought about race not in terms of me being darker than somebody else, but in terms of thinking, 'You know, there's something else about race that's not a good thing.' I didn't think of it in terms of being about my race necessarily, but it struck me that there was this sickness out there that would cause somebody to feel they had to bleach their skin. I couldn't articulate it at the time, I just couldn't. It wasn't like I was able to say to myself, 'Okay, there is a psychology of self-hatred that has been perpetuated.' I wasn't going through all that at six, seven years old. But I do remember feeling like, 'Huh? Well, that's something, that anybody would do this to their own skin, to look lighter.' It was the first time I remember thinking about race in specific terms, in the sense of all the potential negative stereotypes and connotations that go along with race.

"While I became aware then, it probably reached me personally later than most because I was living in Asia and it just wasn't right in my face. My mother was a white woman who just loved black people, loved the civil rights movement. She'd tell me how Harry Belafonte was the best-looking man on the planet. So I had all these positive images. My father was a Harvard-educated man. He was Kofi Annan, except taller. In my mind he was the smartest, most sophisticated person that my maternal grandparents had ever met. So the whole notion that blacks were inferior never came up at the dinner table.

"Then, when I was in high school, I fell into all the stereotypes. I was trying to figure out what it means to be a black man. My father was not in the house, which is true for a lot of young black men, so I didn't have someone in the house saying, 'Ah, that's not what I'm talking about.' I'm playing basketball, I'm getting high, and I'm not taking my work seriously at all. And part of it was because that was what everybody else was doing. If you acted like you were too serious about it, folks would think you were a punk.

"The only things I had going for me was my mother had given me enough values early and I had been a real bookworm when I was younger. So even though there was that period of time during high school when I was acting out, not studying and stuff, I had a good enough foundation that my mother had provided. So I got to college, and I remember some of my teachers saying, 'Man, why are you pretending that you're not smart? Why are you spending all your time on something not serious, instead of focusing on what your talents are?' And, coming from black professors, especially, that was important, because I couldn't throw back at them, 'Oh, you just don't understand.'

"That's a big part of the reason it is so important to have black teachers, especially black male teachers. I'm not saying exclusively, but in many situations you need someone who can call you on your stuff and say exactly what Charles has been talking about, that it's not 'acting white' to read a book. This whole attitude of anti-intellectualism in our communities is one of the most damaging things that we can do to our young people. No other culture I'm aware of does this: tell you it is to your advantage not to be smart. It doesn't make any sense.

"I don't want to exaggerate it. Listen, there are great families who are raising great kids and who are all about work. But there is no doubt that there is pressure there not to achieve academically. And in some of our schools, it can be reinforced in cases where teachers set low expectations. I think it's critical to get kids to understand what is important.

"When I think about how many hours I spent playing ball! Now, as everybody can see, I'm not built like Charles. So, at a certain point, it should have been clear to me, 'The likelihood of you playing in the NBA is not high and, uh, so why don't you spend a little of that time studying Spanish or physics?' "

I thought Barack Obama would be a great person to ask about the choices a biracial child has to make. As I mentioned earlier, my daughter is fifteen years old now, and because her mother is white and

her father is black, she has asked me, "Dad, am I black or am I white?"
And my answer to her is that the question was answered a long, long
time ago for her. Obviously, in this society she's considered black, and
there's no real choice in the matter. Barack has been subject to the
same cultural rules, but as an adult of more than forty years, he does
have the choice now to not allow someone else to define him.

"You go to the cafeteria," Barack said, thinking back to college,
"and the black kids are sitting here, white kids are sitting there, and
you've got to make some choices. For me, basically I could run with
anybody. Luckily for me, largely because of growing up in Hawaii,
there wasn't that sense of sharp divisions. Now, by the time I was ne-
gotiating environments where there were those kinds of sharp divisions, I was already confident enough to make my own decisions. It
became a matter of being able to speak different dialects. That's not
unique to me. Any black person in America who's successful has to be
able to speak several different forms of the same language. You take
on different personas as you need to, when you have to. And there's
nothing wrong with it. It's not unlike a person shifting between Spanish and English. You're going to speak differently on the golf course
with your golf buddies than you are with your cut buddies around the
kitchen table."

Does it make a black person a phony if he changes the way he
speaks around different people? Not at all. It all depends on the situation. I could speak one way among my teammates when the locker
room door was closed, then a totally different way when it opened and
the media came in. Every relationship is different. When you're talking to your preacher, do you use the profanity that might usually pop

up in your speech? Of course you don't. When you talk to your wife, you don't talk to her like you talk to your boys. You don't use the profanity you use around the fellas when you speak in front of your kids.

I don't look at it as phony; I just think it's common sense, adapting to your environment. The one conflict I have is that when I'm with my boys, I use the word "nigger" a lot. Deep in my heart, I wrestle with whether it's a bad word. It has so many negative connotations and was such a tool for repression. I know if a white guy called me a nigger, it's a bad thing. But if one of my black friends said, "Nigga, what's up?" it's cool. I still haven't really reconciled that.

If you're going to try to go back and forth between the black and white worlds, you come into miniconflicts like that all of the time. There are so many gaps between the two cultures, and the burden's always on us as black people to cross them. So many people just quit rather than keep trying.

Of all the things Barack had going for him positively, the most important after having a nurturing mother was understanding sooner than most young black males that valuing education was nothing to be embarrassed over. Even for a kid like Barack, it's never a given. He told us about what happened when he got to that fork in the road.

"Remember, I didn't get serious about my schoolwork, I'd say, until my senior year. That means I had already, to some degree, blown the first three years. But I was smart enough just to be able to get over. However, that's all I did; just get by. We'd have basketball practice get over about six, maybe six-thirty and we'd go get a six-pack and just . . . well, you know. You go to Jack in the Box or something, buy some onion rings and a burger, and go out to the park and just screw around. . . . Then you'd be waking up in the morning and you hadn't done the reading from the night before but, you know, you learned how to talk like you knew what you were talking about. Plus, being charming with the teachers and kinda making them like you, so you could kinda get over a little bit.

"I was doing that whole thing for about three years, and then my senior year in school, I said, 'Man, I should try to go to college, so let me focus a little bit more.' But keep in mind, and this is why I was luckier than most, I'd gotten a scholarship to a prep school, which meant that as much goofing off as I was doing, I was still getting enough of a foundation in education where I wasn't going to fall completely through the cracks. Look, if I'd been on the South Side of Chicago doing the same stuff, I might not have ended up going to college.

"The cracks are so much bigger and so much easier to fall through in big cities where there is so much more to get into that distracts you from education, particularly for children of color. Where I grew up, there were scuffles all the time, right? But you didn't worry about somebody pulling out a gun in the middle of an argument. I mean, that is just not something you were thinking about. What I went through is nothing compared to the kinds of pressures that young African American men, in particular, but also young African American women, are under now.

"I think the dramatic changes, especially in African American communities, poorer African American communities, had partly to do with the crack trade. The economy of the drug industry changed. Until probably the early 1980s, if you wanted to get heroin or almost any of the hard-core drugs, there were a few places you could get it, but it wasn't like having an open-air market. What happened was with the open-air markets, every young kid could start his own business, basically. The question was whether he could be the toughest guy, whether he was willing to do what was necessary to control a corner."

So many people who get into politics have some idea when they're really, really young that they want to do it. Some of them are into public service. Some have parents who, if they aren't involved in politics, are involved in local government. People don't usually just fall into it as a career, but Barack did.

It wasn't until he was well into college that it gradually began to come to him that a life in public service might interest him.

"I started reading more and getting into conversations with professors and I just started looking at the world around me for the first time," Barack said. "I started thinking to myself, 'There is a lot of stuff that is messed up out there. And what's my role in that process, in bringing some sort of change about?' This was about the time when the antiapartheid movement was gaining some momentum in the United States. So, in college, I started getting involved in getting colleges to divest from South Africa. At the time, remember, colleges were investing their money there. South African activists came to the college and I started meeting with them, started planning activities. And I began to feel, 'There is a whole bunch of stuff I've been missing, so let me really buckle down.' So I started studying a lot, focusing a lot on social issues and economics. I became interested in how you bring about change. I became much more of a student of the civil rights movement. It wasn't just the 'I Have a Dream' speech. I started reading about Bob Moses and Fannie Lou Hamer and all these folks that aren't, ya know, always credited, but were just ordinary folks who gave everything they had toward the cause of equal rights.

"They were doing extraordinary things because of the faith they had and the courage they had. So I was really inspired by that, and I said to myself, 'Let me try to devote some time in my life to bringing about change.' But I didn't want to do it through politics. My idea at the time was that I was going to do what the civil rights movement workers had done. I was going to go into communities and organize and work at a grassroots level. So that's what I did. It's how I came to Chicago, actually. I worked in Harlem for a while, but then I came here and was working with a bunch of churches that were trying to deal with steel plants, support workers being laid off. And I worked for three and a half years, being the organizer, before I went to law school.

"And that's really how I got onto a path that led to politics. I'm not one of these guys who thought at the age of seven, 'I wanna be president.' I even thought student council and all that stuff was corny. It just wasn't where I was coming from. My attitude was to see if I could come at it from a grassroots level and help mobilize a movement, and that stayed with me when I went to law school. But then, it stayed with me after law school. I organized a Big Boy Registration Drive. I got 150,000 people registered here in Illinois to help Bill Clinton get elected and Carol Moseley-Braun, who was the last African American U.S. senator. And then I started a civil rights practice and began teaching at the University of Chicago Law School. So it wasn't until 1996, and I was writing my book at the time, when this Senate seat opened up and some people asked me about being a state senator. I said, 'Well, let me see if politics is a way that I can do something.' Still, even as I was considering it, I was suspicious of it, because I was concerned about the corrupting aspects.

"But ultimately, I said, 'Let me get in there and see what can be done.' And over the eight years before this election, I was able to do some good stuff, you know? We reformed a death penalty system that was broken. We had eighteen innocent men on death row in this state. And we changed it so that now when the police arrest somebody on a murder charge, they have to videotape the interrogation and the confession. Otherwise, you can't prove the case. We expanded health care for kids who didn't have it, put more money into the educational system. So after I got by my skepticism, there were concrete things that I was able to accomplish, which is very satisfying. And most of that work, by the way, was accomplished in relative obscurity."

Now, for Barack, that's over. There's no more obscurity, absolute or relative. When you are one of three black U.S. senators since Reconstruction, everybody knows who you are. When you deliver the most talked-about speech during the 2004 Democratic National Convention, everybody knows who you are. The afternoon we talked in his office in Chicago, the award-winning photographer Annie Leibovitz was in a nearby office setting up for a *Vanity Fair* shoot. There's no more alone, especially now that Barack is headed to Washington. There's no more private life, no more working on small-scale voter registration drives. He has no privacy, his wife has no privacy, which might be the one thing I could teach him how to handle.

"I'm not sure I have adapted to it yet," he said. "I'm still getting used to it. I was in Philly to help campaign for John Kerry. I'm just walking down the street in Philly and people are yelling, 'Hey!' But it should be easier for me than athletes or musicians, people who come into this in their early twenties sometimes. I'm forty-three years old and most of my habits are set. My wife is just a funny, down-to-earth, good person. So, the point is we've got a family, we've got a whole way of thinking about stuff. We just step back and it looks like it's happening to somebody else. I don't take myself too seriously. I don't feel like if I lost a political race, it's going to be the end of my life. So my attitude is that the only reason it's worthwhile for me to be in this is . . . is if I can tell the truth."

He doesn't want to talk to people just to tell them what they want to hear. Long before the primary elections, he got together with leaders of the Jewish community with the hopes that they could reestablish the link between African Americans and Jews that was so powerful in the 1960s.

"Above everything else, when I planned to sit and meet with those Jewish leaders, I was going to say what I really thought, what I really felt. And that started with telling them that I care deeply about Israel and I care deeply about the Jewish community. . . . Yet I'm not going to agree with you on everything, and there is going to have to be compromise in terms of resolving some of these problems in the long term. But I'll also say the same thing to Muslims I talk to. I did say the same thing, that I'm not going to agree with everything, but there would have to be some compromise. I'd sit down and tell them, 'I've lived in a Muslim country. I deeply respect your religion. My grandfather was Muslim in Africa, although I never knew him.' But having acknowledged that, I said, 'You still cannot keep on blaming somebody else for things that you guys aren't handling the way they should be handled.' And I'll say the same things to black folks and I'll say the same thing to white folks. Now, what I do try to do, and I think this is something that's important, is to make sure they know that I'm listening. People can be quick to take offense on issues of race and culture, and they have to feel like you're listening if you're going to even address the issue. You can't just be in their face.

"So while I will talk about issues that are of high concern to black voters, for example, in predominantly white audiences, I'm not going to get in their faces and say, 'Look at these terrible things you are doing to me.' What I'm a lot more likely to say is, 'Look at this injustice and what can we—as people of goodwill—do to solve the injustice?' I'm simply not going to come at them with, 'I'm the victim and you're the perpetrator.' I'm going to come at them saying, 'We have a problem here and how can we work together to solve it?' And I believe that's the kind of tone in politics I want to set because a big part of the problem we've got now is people just yelling at each other."

That's a primary concern of mine, too, and one of the primary reasons I wanted to engage people in this kind of dialogue, because usually the dialogue is forced by some ugly, if not tragic, incident. And at that point, the dialogue is buried in a whole lot of rhetoric and hurt feelings and anger, and nobody's listening. I'm a politics junkie. I watch probably far too many of the political talk shows. And what irks me after a while is it all boils down to the fact that one is liberal, one is conservative. They yell at each other for half an hour and nothing gets solved. They've made money for thirty minutes of talk. The network has made money. The show's sponsors have invaded my living room for thirty minutes or an hour, and we're no closer to solving anything. I always watch, and at the end I always wind up saying, "What just happened here?" And it's such a scam the way it works. I don't think I can necessarily solve anything, but I think we're better

**served by some kind of rational discussion. Otherwise, as Barack
said, "It's a circus. It's entertainment."**

"Part of what I really wanted to do with my campaign for the Senate and part of what I want to do as a United States senator is to take
politics back from that kind of circus atmosphere. And just say, 'You
know what? This is serious business. These are people's lives we're
talking about.'

"I wind up using a sports analogy here all the time," Barack continued. "You can compete and compete hard. But there must be a way
of competing hard and yet respectfully. In a sense, you know the rules
of the game; some of them are unwritten and some of them are written. But there is a way for you to go back and forth with somebody
that's not 'I'm going to take your knees out.' Right? And what we have
is a political atmosphere right now where people don't mind, when
you're going for a layup, cutting under you and taking your legs completely out from under you. You don't play that stuff.

"That is part of what I see too much of in politics. It's what we saw
too much of with John Kerry before the 2004 presidential election.
You can argue with him about his foreign policies. You can certainly
say he wasn't right to throw away his medals and criticize people when
he got back. But to accuse him of not getting shot at and to just out-
and-out lie about a guy's war record when you're making the criticism
and you don't even have a war record. There's too much anything
goes and no holds barred. I think it's damaging. We've seen this
yelling and disparaging. It can't solve anything in a nation divided
and it solves even less when you're talking about the issue of race.

"The thing that I'm absolutely convinced about is that you cannot solve problems and issues pertaining to race just by yelling. I mean, it's got to be a dialogue where you're appealing to what Abraham Lincoln called 'the better angels of people's natures.' You're talking to them and finding what's best in them. Look, I'm sure there's not a black person who has not had the experience of being with some-body white who is basically a good person, but says something igno-rant. I mean, you're sitting with somebody you know to be fundamentally a good person, and yet that person will say some-thing that offends or that reflects an ignorance about you or an en-tire race of people.

"Well, you can respond in a couple of ways, right? You can start just yelling and stop interacting. Or you can say to yourself, 'I know this guy is actually a decent person, so let's see if I can work this through with him so that we can still have a relationship.' I think that's my gen-eral approach. Listen, I know there are some folks who are hard-core racists. They're not going to change and I'm not going to waste my time with them. But the majority of the American people, I person-ally believe, don't mean black folks ill."

As a southerner, somebody who has seen segregation just this side of Jim Crow, I agree with that entirely. I know there are some KKK members who are going to hate the sight of black folks until they die. But I think the great majority of white people don't even know any-body black. I have some experience with this because I run into peo-ple who see me on television, and because they feel like they know me, they'll start to talk openly about not knowing any black people and their primary exposure is what they see on television, where we are portrayed in some really unflattering ways. I think the majority of white people can go either way. Too often, all they see is athletes or

entertainers. That's the only exposure . . . or black people playing roles that are stereotypical.

"They're just trying to take care of their own business," Barack said. "Basically, what they don't want is somebody yelling at them, making them feel bad, when they're not even thinking about most of this stuff. Now, on the flip side, I firmly believe the overwhelming majority of African Americans are just as hardworking, just as intent to go about their business as well. What is true, though, is sometimes I think we get into the mode of it's easier to blame white folks for things than us taking the responsibility. That is the flip side of the coin. At some point we know we have to take responsibility. Nobody is forcing parents to not look after their children.

"Obviously, in some situations, there is a lot of poverty. And it's a lot more difficult. But our grandparents were poorer than that and they looked after their children. Poverty didn't strip our ancestors of their sense of responsibility."

In many ways, because of his age and the alliances he has formed across racial lines, Barack Obama is a transitional figure in politics. But still, he will be described first and foremost as a black politician. Even as his story is told and retold, even as people point out that his mother is white, he will never outlive the description that he is a black politician. And one of the cool things I found about him is that even while he embraces everybody and has succeeded in being more inclusive than most of his counterparts, he still understands the history and legacy of the important black political figures who came before him, who made it possible for him. One month after our visit in his Chicago office, he won a U.S. Senate seat in a landslide victory.

Not only blacks but whites are talking about him being a presidential candidate in 2012, when he would still be only fifty-one years old.

"We all stand on the shoulders of others," Barack said. "And, so, if Harold Washington doesn't become mayor and go through what he went through at some of these neighborhoods, getting spat on and yelled at and cursed, if Jesse Jackson doesn't run for president, then Carol Moseley-Braun doesn't get elected as U.S. senator. And if Carol Moseley-Braun doesn't get elected to the U.S. Senate, all these things, then I probably don't even have the opportunity to run for the Senate. What we have to do is build this bridge into our future brick by brick. Everybody is trying to add to that bridge. And our kids then follow and move in a better direction.

"I can see how far it has come, the building of the bridge, because I arrived here in '85, about a year and a half after the big Council Wars. This was when Harold Washington and the white city council were just going at it, every single day, apparently. And every single day it was about race. I mean, every day it was black folks and white folks going at each other. Every day, in the newspapers, on TV, in meetings. You couldn't get away from it. It was almost impossible for Harold to do anything. They were just blocking it up and, to some of them, it wasn't even personal. From their perspective, Harold had come in and was dismantling the political machine that had existed for decades and decades. And this, to them, was about their jobs and contracts. The best way for some of them to fight the changes, the reform he was attempting, was to stir the racial pot. At the same time, for perhaps the first time, there were black folks who had the perspective that 'this is our turf now.'

"That's when I first came to Chicago. And what is true, and also satisfying when you look at the climate today, is that one of my opponents [in the Democratic primary] was a very fine young man named Dan Hynes, who is the Illinois State Comptroller, a statewide elected official. He is the son of Tom Hynes, who ran against Harold in 1987. Dan Hynes had all the support of all the old ward guys on the southwest side and the northwest side. And what was satisfying in the race was that we won in all those wards against one of their own. . . . I mean, we defeated the favorite son. That said a lot about the progress we had made in less than twenty years. It also said a lot about Dan Hynes, because he was very classy in that race and he never tried to play the race card with me. He was always a very respectful opponent and was fully supportive after the race. His whole family, which controlled the nineteenth ward, has been very supportive. They all came behind my campaign.

"One of my favorite sayings is from Dr. Martin Luther King: 'The arc of the whole universe is long but it bends toward justice.' It takes a long time for us to sometimes step back and see the progress that's being made. But when we are able to step back, we can see that progress really is being made."

We could see the progress when Obama stood onstage at the Democratic convention. To have a black man in such a prominent position, giving the keynote speech, was huge. He won his Senate seat by an overwhelming majority in a predominantly white state in the Midwest.

And as we sat with him, I thought, "This is the guy who can lead our people."

I know he has even larger goals, that he wants to unite, to bring the races closer together. I just think there is so much mistrust that's been taught to white people and black people, and there's so much financial segregation, that it's going to be difficult. And then poor white people are taught to hate poor black people, rather than banding together to get better schools, more security. We spend so much time fighting each other.

Barack can bring people together. It won't be enough to get him elected president of the United States, but it would sure be something. Personally, I don't think America will ever have a black president. The racial divide runs too deep. But Barack will be a good test if he does run for the Oval Office. If America can't find him qualified and appealing enough to elect, that would tell you just about everything you need to know. But I don't want to limit the focus—and our perception of him—to that one question.

Instead of asking what Barack Obama can become, we should ask ourselves what we can do to become more like Barack Obama.

ACTING
BLACK
SAMUEL L.
JACKSON

Sam Jackson is one of America's greatest actors, as well as one of the most prolific. He has appeared in nearly ninety films, from starring roles in box-office hits to roles in which he asked for and received no screen credit. One point he made over and over in our discussion over lunch in Beverly Hills was that he loves to work. He loved to act on the stage and now loves to act in movies. In 1990, he appeared in seven movies, including *Mo' Better Blues*, *The Exorcist III*, and *Goodfellas*. He has played roles as diverse as Charles Morritz in *The Red Violin* and the infamous Jules Winnfield in *Pulp Fiction*, but at this point he never plays the same character twice.

Sam is one of a handful of black actors who has roles occasionally written for him, but who can and does say no if he doesn't like a part. He doesn't audition anymore. He doesn't play characters who are killed off early, unless he wants to. He has the ability, unlike the great Sidney Poitier before him, to pick and choose his roles and still have plenty of satisfying work. He has the chance to become the richest actor in American film history. Yet he can quickly summon up the feeling of what it was like to cash a check so small from his work in the theater that the bank teller looked at him like he was a chump.

Because he has seen everything the movie industry has had to offer, Sam was the perfect person to talk to about race in the film industry, about not just his own ability to successfully negotiate an industry that is only now becoming moderately inclusive when it comes to black folks, but the industry and its relationship with black folks period.

For him, moviemaking begins with storytelling.

"I learned about storytelling first and foremost from my grandfather," Sam said, "because I used to sit on the porch with him when I was a kid. He and I were the only two men in the house, so we bonded because all those women were always on us and I was the only child. If anything got broke, weren't no dogs, weren't no cats to blame, none of that. It was me getting a whipping. My grandfather always told me stories: horror stories, stories about his childhood, jokes, funny stories. I heard stories all my life from my uncles and my grandfather and his brothers—all great storytellers. They sat around on the porch at night drinking moonshine and beer and telling stories. We didn't have a TV for a long time when I was a kid, so we listened to radio: Andy Griffith, who was a great storyteller, as well as 'Sgt. Preston of the Yukon,' 'Amos 'N Andy,' all on the radio. My facility for listening and repeating became really great.

"I also learned how to make up stories to tell my cousins and friends. I was by myself, so I lived in my head a lot and read. I've been able to read since I was, like, three, and my mom always insisted that I read books. So I immersed myself in books, and for every four comic books I read, I had to read a classic. I've been hidden in a book all my life.

"Of course, I also went to the movies. Now, mind you, I grew up in the segregated South, so we had black theaters. Every Saturday I was at the movies all day. We used bags from a Lays potato chip promotion to get into the movies, so you had all these black kids going to the movies with shopping bags full of potato chip bags. They had cartoons from nine to twelve o'clock; then they'd have the monster movie or the western or the war picture double feature. After being at the movies all day long, I'd come back home and act out the movies to my friends. Also, my aunt, who lived with us, was a performing arts teacher, and when she had to do pageants and plays, there were never enough boys, so she made me perform. I had a costume on all my life.

"Growing up in Tennessee, of course I grew up in segregation, so I've always been very aware of race issues. I once let a white girl up on our front porch, and my grandmother and two aunts beat the crap out of me. 'That's something that'll get you killed!' I was about four, maybe five when that happened. I just saw this little white girl walking down the street. It was a white girl; it wasn't even a white woman.

"But that was part of the education of growing up in the South. There are things that will get you killed. I was told very early on about speaking a certain way to white people. You always said, 'Yes sir, no sir,' no matter who they were. I would go to work with my grandfather, 'cause he was this janitor for like four different places, including a law firm and a real estate firm. These old guys were smoking cigars all day long, supreme rednecks but rich rednecks, and I had to learn to talk to them in a specific kind of way, be kind of deferential. I would watch my grandfather, just kind of clock what he was doing and do that. You learned when you went downtown the places you could go and the places you couldn't go, the things you could say and the things you couldn't say, the things you were not supposed to touch unless there was someone there watching you. And my whole education was black, all my teachers, everybody I went to school with. The only time I interacted with white people was when I went to town or did things like Model United Nations. I was a smart kid so I did stuff like that. And I did UNICEF meetings and World Congress kind of things where they were trying to make kids of various races interact. Other than that, my whole existence was black."

Growing up in segregated Alabama, I also spent my childhood surrounded by black people. Then I got to Auburn, where the majority of the campus was white, and I found it to be a great experience. I was better prepared for life in the real world because of that exposure. I'm always surprised that even after the battles fought from the lunch counters to the courtrooms to integrate America, many black people still choose to stay separate.

The way I see it is, you've got to be comfortable in both the white world and the black world to exist. You're not going to get stuff done in just the black world because you're going to have to go into the white world to work. That's just how it is. You're going to have to re-

late to white people in the majority of workplaces. White people've got to relate better to us, and we've got to relate better to them.

One of the messages Sam wanted to get out in *A Time to Kill* was just how separate his character's life was from that of Matthew McConaughey's character. In one scene he tells Matthew, "We're not friends. You go to work, you're nice to me, I'm nice to you, but you've never even been to my house." I think most white and black relationships in this country are like that. A white person can't be my friend if he doesn't come to my house, hang out with my kid, something like that. We go to dinner, we go to work together, but if it ends there, we're not friends. We're just co-workers, or maybe associates. And if black people and white people are working together, it's usually on white people's terms. It definitely was that way for Sam when he first got to Hollywood.

"For a while, if you were black, you were always the bad guy," he said. "Pick up a script and see what crime I did and which page I died on. That's what went on. The world was fine because we can kill them. Even though on television, Avery Brooks played Hawk on 'Spenser: For Hire,' he was a different kind of character. He lived in the underworld but Spenser needed him because he could negotiate Spenser through different things. He was essentially a bad guy who was there to do bad things to bad guys because he was badder than the bad guys in a certain kind of way. He had a moral compass that was different from ours.

"Characters changed to a degree due to integration. People who write and produce go to school with people of different ethnic groups. They have friends who are black or Asian or Hispanic. So when people who have had more diverse lives write, they see doctors and lawyers as black or Hispanic or Asian. A long time ago those writers didn't have those kinds of contacts. They didn't have black friends or Asian friends or Hispanic friends. So when they wrote, they wrote in the consciousness of the society that they dwelled in. When you went to be cast, even though you were perfect for the doctor role, or you were well spoken, it was like, you know, 'There ain't no white people who want a black doctor! The other people in the story are white and they're not going to be treated by you so we're not going to even entertain that idea.' But now that's different to a great degree. There are black surgeons, black lawyers, black cops now. Whereas before even the black cops were sort of bad cops. Because they did stuff to the niggas that they didn't do to the white people. They come in and beat the brothers down, you know. While the white cops stood there and watched them beat them down because they were blue before they were black. And now you have a different kind of consciousness in the television-watching audience and in the moviegoing audience . . . because integration changed all of that and because of hip-hop.

"When I got 'discovered,' I was a crackhead, and I was playing Gator in *Jungle Fever* so I had that covered. But because I had done so much theater I also knew that I wasn't going to be playing crackheads the rest of my life, that there were other things that I could do and things that I wanted to do, so I made a conscious effort to go from a crackhead to the next film, *White Sands,* which was at the total opposite end of the spectrum. In it, I played a guy who was well respected, college-educated, wore a suit . . . still a bad guy, but with a different agenda. I have a need—and my agents and managers know that particular need—to be a different guy every time I show up. I could have played Jules till the end of my career. The character's so cool that all of a sudden after *Pulp Fiction* I became the coolest actor in Hollywood 'cause I played a guy who was cool. But I choose to do things like read a script and say, 'I don't want to be that guy, I want to be *this* guy.' And that particular guy might be somebody producers and writers haven't even considered being African American."

It's cool to see someone like Sam achieve that kind of clout, where he can turn down roles, or choose different characters than the ones he's offered. That's real power.

I'll pass on a commercial endorsement if it seems offensive to me. When I was eighteen or nineteen, I might have done it, but now I won't do just anything. In the spring of 2004, when ABC offered me a chance to join the announcing team of "Monday Night Football," that wasn't "just anything." The Monday Night Football booth is the most coveted territory in sportscasting, and I was honored to be given a chance to join the longest-running, highest-rated show in prime-time sports. It would have been huge.

But as I talked about it with my friends, some of them told me it would be just as huge to be able to turn it down. I was torn, because it was an incredible opportunity. But I wasn't sure I wanted to spend even more time on the road away from my daughter than I already did. And I wasn't sure I could really make that much of a difference with the already great broadcasting team of Al Michaels and John Madden.

So I can appreciate that Sam has the luxury of saying no, of refusing to play the same old roles: the bad guy, the funny guy. One thing that annoys me about Hollywood is how when they put black people on television, we've got to be funny. We've got to be comedians and stuff like that. Look at "Soul Food," the black family drama. They don't even put it on network television. It had to go to cable on Show-

time. We don't have any black dramas on network TV. We're either comedians or we're entertaining, singing and stuff. It's not like we can't
do any great acting—and anyway, look at all of those crappy other
shows—but all black people get are comedies. And that's only after
they throw a show out there every couple of years because we start
complaining. When a black man does get the lead role on a show,
he's a comedian: from the days of Redd Foxx to Bill Cosby to Damon
Wayans and Bernie Mac. We can't have any romances. Or dramas.
We've got to make jokes and make everybody laugh.

Then, when we make good movies, it's a "black movie." You never
hear movies with all-white casts described as "white movies."

I joke with my friends who are in movies with all-black casts: "Until
you make a movie with some white people in it, you'll never be a
movie star; you're just an actor." But, sadly enough, it's true. It's
tough to shed that black-movie-actor tag. Even those black actors who
have crossed over can't keep that label from being applied to their
films if they have a black director.

"Movies like *Ray* are not considered black movies," Sam said. "It's
not, interestingly enough, though it's about a black character, just
like *Ali* was not considered a black movie because Michael Mann directed it. If you've got a white British director, it's not a black movie.
If you've got a black star and a black director and a black subject, then
it's a black movie. Some people probably called *Coach Carter,* my
movie that came out in January of 2005, a 'black movie' because it
stars me, it's about a black basketball team, and it was directed by a
black man. But it's about a universal subject: education. It's not essentially about basketball; it's about a guy who made his basketball
players sign a contract saying they would keep a certain GPA, that

they would go to class every day. But guys on game days didn't do this and when he found out they weren't doing it, he shut the team down. They were undefeated . . . the team wins everything, true story.

"The movie tested through the roof. People loved it because of the subject matter and because it's about something. But the pressure is always the same on everybody. The pressure is for the movie to open and have legs. Then a greater pressure is: Can it make money internationally?

"When Denzel Washington makes a movie, it has international possibilities. That matters because these guys make all their money on how the movie does around the world. They hope to pay their production costs with the domestic money, and the profit comes internationally. When your movie opens around the world and makes money, then you become viable to Hollywood. All my films become viable to Hollywood because all of them make money around the world. No matter what country I go into, people know who I am and they go to my movies. I was just in Japan where most people don't even know black actors, but they knew who I was. I go out and promote my films. I go to Germany, France, the U.K., Brazil, Spain, Japan, Australia; I don't care where it is, I go. And people respect you more because you show up and you're on the local television shows and they think you care about your product and you care about them because you came there to say to them, 'Please come out and see my movie.'

"In order to become viable, you have to be an international box-office star. George Lucas just told me that if I reach $175 million next year, before Harrison Ford releases another film, I'll be the highest grossing actor in the history of movies. Between *The Incredibles* and *Star Wars* I should be able to do that. Plus they said, 'We'll put you in

Indiana Jones, so Harrison will never catch you again.' George says that I am addicted to work. You get up every day and you just show up and you work. You don't make distinctions between big roles, small roles. I read scripts and if I like the story I'll say, 'Well I don't have time to do twelve weeks, but I'd like to do this part right here. I can go in and bounce that and knock that out and do it . . . because I want to be in the movie, because I think the movie is viable.' Now sometimes I'll just do a movie and say, 'I don't want to be credited.' I do it because I like the story and I just want to be part of it. That happened with *Kill Bill.* Quentin Tarantino and I have that kind of relationship."

When people talk about stars who have the ability to transcend race, what they really mean is, if you're a black guy, you've got to be the nicest guy in the world. You've got to be a nice guy all the time. Barry Bonds doesn't transcend race, for example. Even though he's the best baseball player of our time, he still isn't loved by white America. It's kind of unfair.

Sam thinks movie actors start with a greater benefit of the doubt.

"People go to movies because they want to be excited by what they see on the screen," Sam said. "They want to be excited by the story. They don't care who's in it, they don't care what color the people are, and they don't read reviews. We read them because we're intelligent people who want to be informed about another way of watching a film or want to make an informed choice. The person they make movies for, the fourteen- to twenty-five-year-olds, they're going to movies because they watched the trailer or their friends say, 'Man, that movie is the bomb, you gotta go see it.' "

It's the freedom to not only choose and reject work, but to help projects make it to the screen that black and Hispanic folks have not realized, even though they go to the movies and watch television in disproportionate numbers. If it's a handful of black actors who can carry a film or be "viable," then you can count on one hand the number of blacks who can get a project made. That's a kind of creative freedom that blacks still largely don't enjoy.

"For years," Sam said, "we ran around with *Eve's Bayou,* and nobody got it. The big problem was it's a black family drama. 'Where's the car exploding?' people would say. 'Where's the gun? Where's the sex?' Granted, it's hard to get a white family drama done, too. That's why those stories are all independent films. You get a minimum amount of money to go in and you hope you can do them for a little money and then make a lot of money because it garners interest or word of mouth or it's just so dynamic that it happens. Like *My Big Fat Greek Wedding.* There's one, but maybe no more than that, every year.

"I had an issue with HBO way back when. I had read this book about a brother who started a town. He left the Louisiana bayou, went to World War I. He and some brothers ran up on some Germans raping a girl, saved the girl's life, protected this town, and they found all this gold that the Germans had stashed in this town. They smuggled it back to the United States, and this Jewish cat helped them turn it into cash and they started buying nightclubs and all this other stuff and then he started building a black town. At the same time HBO was doing 'The Corner.' And I was like, what's the counter programming to 'The Corner'? You know, all the brothers shooting dope and calling each other motherfuckers and niggers and killing each other all over television. Here I got a cat that's a positive role model and they say it's a little too violent for us! I said, it ain't 'Oz'! There *are* some positive things that black men do. Plus it's historical. They said, 'Well, we don't want to do a period piece.' And then they do 'Deadwood.' I'm like, excuse me? Help me understand this. They don't have explanations for it. They just make up shit. 'It's too violent, it's too this.' But then they're doing something that is just as violent."

As great as it is that, in some cases, Sam has the influence to help shape what makes it to the big screen, it's difficult to have this conversation with him without thinking of the black actors and actresses, from Paul Robeson to Lena Horne to Ossie Davis to Sidney Poitier, who had the same passion to work and the same instincts about how black folks are portrayed or excluded completely. Far too many times in professional sports, young athletes don't know the men and women who preceded them, who blazed the trail to help make a sport popular, or make it attractive for TV so that advertisers and money would flow into the game. But Sam doesn't just have a sense of those who preceded him; in many cases, he's intimately familiar with the work and has a great sense of how bumpy the road was before people like Poitier paved it.

"Sidney and I play golf and we talk about all kinds of stuff," Sam said. "He talks to me about the business, how I've conducted myself, the things that I've done and how proud he is that I've diversified myself, and about being a very different kind of actor than he was. But I used to ask my mom all the time, 'Why does he die in the movies?' My first real vivid image is *Edge of the City,* with John Cassavetes, when they're fighting with these bale hooks and Sidney's got him. But instead of killing Cassavetes, Sidney messed him up and they start all over again. Then Sidney misses and falls. . . . And Cassavetes hooks Sidney in the back. I'm sitting there as a kid thinking, 'What the hell happened here?' Then, in *The Long Ships,* it's the same thing. He's got Richard Widmark, got him down, got the sword to his neck. Lets him up . . . bell comes down and crushes his ass. I'm like 'What's going on?' And it wasn't until I started working that I realized why Sidney's characters were always dying. 'Cause, back then, you got to kill the nigger. The world isn't going to be safe unless the nigger's dead."

As bad as it seems some years, when it's difficult to find a black character who isn't pimpin' or killing somebody or dealing drugs, black actors know how far the industry has come. At least it's gotten to the point where there's not just one cattle call audition for bad guys.

"I remember going to an audition for *Sneakers,* which starred Robert Redford," Sam said. "That was one of the first auditions that I went to out in Los Angeles. It was so funny because it was me, and I was in my thirties, plus some older brothers. All we knew was there was a call for a 'black character,' so you had all age ranges in there. My wife tells me that when she goes to auditions still, they have her, they have all these young black girls, these hoochie girls with the short stuff on, then they have some older black women. They don't know what they want. All they know is the character is black.

"I don't go to auditions now, but in the past when I'd go to auditions with cornrows, it wouldn't even be worth being there. Usually I had a goatee or a mustache, I had an Afro. I knew I wasn't getting any kind of commercial. That just wasn't happening. I couldn't sell soup. I couldn't sell soap. I didn't look like the dude with two cars, a dog, and a wife. Now, brothers have cornrows on in the beer commercials. They're trying to sell beer to those brothers, you know? Now, the undercover cop has got cornrows, goatees. They have baggy shirts, baggy pants, and the criminal is a white boy now, trying to be black, hanging with the brothers, trying to get some drugs.

"Did you ever think you would hear James Brown's or Rick James's music selling a damn car? A white guy is driving down the street in a new sedan and 'Super Freak' is playing, and they're trying to sell you a car. How the hell did that happen? Even McDonald's is using rap songs, all these brothers selling cell phones, selling Sprite. We've infiltrated the culture in such a way that they realize that white kids in the suburbs want to be Cube, want to be Ludacris. The white kids who go to the malls every week, they buy that stuff up. They're appealing to them through our music and our images because that's who they want to be. They bought right into the whole thing because brothers are cool. These little Jewish kids would come to my house to see my daughter when she was in high school. They come in saying to me, 'What up, Dog?' And I'm saying to them, 'Hey, kid, does your mama know you're black?' "

There's no question that Sam Jackson is about the coolest of the black actors. For that matter, he's one of the coolest actors regardless of color, and it's mostly because of a role he played—Jules, in _Pulp Fiction_ with John Travolta and Uma Thurman, a movie that underscored how viable he is as an actor and proved that moviegoers don't give a damn who is in the movies. What matters is whether a producer will broaden the viewer's thinking enough to be inclusive when it comes to casting.

"When I read that script for *Pulp Fiction*," Sam recalls, "I was in Virginia doing an HBO movie about Johnson C. Whittaker. I had had lunch with Quentin and he told me he was writing this thing for me. He sent it to me, I'm sitting in the room, I read the script, and I was like, 'Goddamn, this is incredible.' It was so incredible I didn't believe it. I went back to the beginning and read it all over again. I was like 'I love this, and I have friends who will go and see this movie.' But nobody is going to let him make this movie. Well, maybe Miramax. If they leave him alone and let him make what's on the page, it will change how people look at movies. And sure enough they did. Now, who knew it was going to have the crossover appeal that it had? I just thought it was audience-specific. People like me who smoked dope and guys who had a street mentality—they would see it as what it was, just like a ghetto opera. But suddenly it crossed over and I didn't realize that until I was at the Cannes Film Festival and we're sitting there the first night, watching the movie, and the people were loving the hell out it, and then I realize, they're reading it in French. The majority of them aren't even getting what the movie is about 'cause they're reading it in French. And that's when I knew. I said, 'This is just going to rock.' Sure enough, it did.

"After that, I realized I could actually resist doing the same role when my manager told me that 'no' is the most powerful word you can hear in Hollywood. She says the more you say no, the more they want you. So I just kept refusing to do it, every time Jules came back, I'd just say, 'No.' Every time Gator came back, 'No.' No. The biggest influence on me was when Lawrence Olivier died and I was watching his eulogy and they put his face up on the screen and talked about him and he started to morph from one character to the next. I was sitting there thinking, 'Damn, you can actually do that?' That's why

I reinvent myself in movie after movie after movie. I was so glad when I discovered this wigmaker because you know hair makes people. I've come through eight different generations of hairstyles and I call on those. I see people on the street, I'll take a picture of them, or I'll have my hairdresser Robert take a picture. His sister's hair was my hair in *The Negotiator*. I did a film with a guy in South Africa last year. I loved his hair and used it in a film I did in Toronto last year, *The Minors*. You keep reinventing yourself in different kinds of ways and finding stories that have characters on the inside of them that allow you to change.

"The character I play in *A Time to Kill* was straight-up one of those country cats I used to go and spend time with in Rome, Georgia. You know, pigeon-toed, change your walk, change your posture, let your hair grow . . . you know, a working stiff. But I still have issues with that movie. When you read the book, the story is essentially about a guy who had to do what the white people do to the brothers in the movies all the time. He had to kill those two white cats so that his daughter would know that no matter what goes on in this world, if anything happens to her she is protected. When I shot the movie, that's what my whole focus was. We shot all the stuff from when I go to the lawyer the first time and I start talking to him about these guys. I actually tell him the story of what happened to her, that whole story that Matthew McConaughey tells at the end of the movie. But when I saw the movie the first time, my scene was gone! Then there's another scene where I talk to him about my brother and why I had to kill these guys. I explain why I had to protect her, that the world has got to be safe. That scene? Gone. So all of a sudden it becomes Carl Lee Hailey's revenge story. Changed the whole tone of who the character was. That's when you find out what happens in the editing world. I was a little naive about it.

"This was Matthew McConaughey's first picture. He told me when I met him, 'It's just such an honor to be working with you.' I was like, 'Yeah, I heard a lot about you. I hear you're the new golden boy.' He said, 'No, no, I'm just here to learn.' And I told him, 'You know what, you'll make more than I will on the next movie. As long as I've been working, you'll get paid three times as much as I do the next movie.'

"Anyway, with them cutting those scenes, that's an instance of an Oscar lost because you know Oscars are won and lost on moments in films. It's a particular moment that the audience just can't let go. It has nothing to do with the whole performance.

"Denzel didn't just get to be great at what he does when he won an Oscar for his performance in *Training Day*. It was just so stunning to some people to see him play a bad guy. People looked at his performance and said, 'We've never seen Denzel this way before! What a departure . . . Oh my God; he's playing a nigger!'

"When Halle Berry and Denzel won the Oscars for Best Actress and Best Actor, they were the two best performances that year and they should have won. There have been years when more than two African Americans won awards, but they weren't in the most high profile categories and people didn't realize that the people who won for sound or short films and other stuff were African Americans. So I was happy for Halle and Denzel. But I wasn't thinking, 'Oh my God, we broke through.' I don't buy into that divide-and-conquer bull. Someone asked me about a job that Denzel got: 'Do you feel like so-and-so gets better roles than you do?' No. Because my opinion is that everybody does what they're supposed to do. You make your own space. Tom

Cruise isn't mad at Tom Hanks 'cause he's making movies each year. And Tom Cruise and Tom Hanks aren't mad at John Travolta because he made some huge movie. There's room for all of them. Same thing for us. There's enough room for all of us here, too. There's plenty of space. I'm a little mad because Morgan doesn't have an Academy Award and he deserves one. He should have had two, probably three. In *The Nutty Professor* Eddie Murphy successfully played six people. If a white actor does that, they'd be like 'Oh God!' Denzel definitely should have won for *Hurricane*. I should have won for *Pulp Fiction, Jackie Brown,* and *Jungle Fever.* Morgan should have won the first time he got nominated, in *Street Smart.* He scared the crap out of Christopher Reeve, who was looking at him like, 'Where the hell did y'all find this nigger? I think he's a real pimp.' "

You sit there and listen to a famous, wealthy, celebrated black actor, and it somehow sounds just about the same as talking to a black teacher or accountant or construction worker in the sense that it's still a struggle to receive acclaim, even for the best work. You get reminded that people of color almost never are in a position to control perception or production. You're still waiting for someone else—okay, whites in authority positions—to make the evaluations and have the final word on how you're going to be perceived, or whether you're going to work this year. And because that process is rarely questioned in the entertainment industry, it never seems to change.

"It's just the nature of the beast. It's their business," Sam said, almost matter-of-factly. "Occasionally, I had the luxury, I guess, sort of a luxury, of being part of the Spike Lee film count, so for like three summers, we would get together and work for Spike. It was essentially a black set and it worked fine, but the majority of times that's not going to be the case, so you learn to deal with it. You surround yourself with as many people as you can who are very competent, and when you meet people who are competent, you recommend them for the next job or the next job or the next job. I have a black assistant, I have a black hairdresser, I had a black makeup artist but she decided to do something else so I got this other white guy, well, he's Italian so we always told him he was an honorary brother. Al, my dresser, is black, usually my drivers are black, there are a lot of really good black soundmen who have won or been nominated for Academy Awards. I try to get friends of mine who are very efficient people, who can keep track of things and write things, I try to get them to learn to be script supervisors, keeping up with what the shot was, what lens was used, how far away they were. They're in charge of continuity. It's a great job. You work every day.

"Most of the time people just want to be on camera because that's the thing they see. It's the only thing they're aware of. It's the glamour. But the people behind the scenes can be just as rich. Now, there are some things, like when you try to get into the Teamsters Union, that are difficult, because they're a mom-and-pop kind of organization. You might have to be brought in by a family member—you're automatically eligible if your daddy or uncle or whoever is already there—but if you're black somebody's got to invite you and some other people have to vouch for you and that doesn't happen that often. That's a really closed shop, and they make so much money it's crazy. But there are a whole lot of jobs available: sound guys, grips, light technicians, drivers, camera operators, guys who pull focus. There are all these jobs available in an industry that pays lucrative salaries that people don't know about. If you like making movies, people say they want to be directors, okay fine. But if not, learn how to operate the camera, learn how to lower the film, learn about the lights. Learn all these different things that will give you an opportunity to do all these different jobs.

"When I did *Country of My Skull* in South Africa, we used a black crew that knew exactly what they were doing. The major players came from Ireland and England, but they were instructed to hire South Africans to work—some they had to teach, some were already capable. You try and do it as often as you possibly can because you want more people to know the business. But in the end, you always have to have a good product. I hate that attitude of 'Well, you know, this is just a little black movie.' That doesn't mean it's supposed to be bad! It needs to be a good little black movie and it needs to look good, it needs to have good dialogue, it needs to be cut well. It needs to be all those things.

"I've always been very comfortable with being who I am and I make sure that my character makes sense for me, from a small thing like the robber in *Coming to America* to things I do now. Because of the way I was trained and because of the way I approach the work, people accept the things that I bring, and if they make sense for me racially, they make sense for me in a human nature sort of way and they make sense for me as a member of an audience going to watch the film. So consequently, I don't have problems watching my films. I watch them all the time. I like watching. All the years I was doing theater, I wanted to watch the play I was in but I wanted to watch it with me in it. So this affords me the opportunity to watch myself do what I really love to do.

"There's something right about people who work, and there's something wrong about people who don't. When they look at your résumé, and say, 'Wow, you have three jobs,' they want to hire you, too. You know that other cat that ain't worked in a year? Hmmm, 'Okay, it's been nice seeing you.' Success breeds success. Today, I have boxes and boxes and boxes of the neatest sneakers because my mom couldn't afford to buy me a pair of Converse when I was a poor kid in Tennessee. All I wanted was the Chuck Taylors; everybody had them but I didn't. They cost $11! That wasn't happening. Now I make more on one movie than my mother made in her whole life. When I think about the amounts of money my grandfather and my grand- mother worked for and what they did with it, how they raised a fam- ily on it . . . and compare it to the amounts of money I get paid to do what I do, all I can do is kind of smile. I sit in that room with those people and say, 'You're not messing with me, you know who you're messing with. I hate you, I hate you, I'm going to do the job but I hate you, I hate you.' And then I get in my car and I can't help but laugh, man. I mean I work ten weeks for $5 million. You know, people will be like, 'I'm not doing ten weeks for $5 million.' They must be crazy. Sure I will."

It reminds me of my final year with the Rockets. We couldn't sign Scottie Pippen unless I took a pay cut, so I took a $5 million pay cut. The Rockets said, "You know what? We're going to make it up for you, we're going to give you $12 million. It's going to be a going away present." I'm thinking, "That's mighty nice." So I get there, day be- fore training camp starts and they tell me, "Well, we changed our mind; we're going to give you $9 million." I say, "You mothers, screw y'all. I want my $12 million." They tell me, "You have no other choice; it's too late now." I'm screaming, "Man, screw you, screw you and all your families. . . . Give me that pen." We laughed about it.

"Hey, Charles, I know you played in the sun, in the dust," Sam said. "You did everything you were supposed to do to get where you had to get. I struggled. I jumped the turnstile to auditions. I worked for $90 for a six-month run or whatever. I worked every theater in the country. And yeah, I had my own little pity party. I was smoking cocaine, I used the excuse that Charles Dutton was doing a role that I had done—*The Piano Lesson.* The role was written for him and the only reason he wasn't doing it initially was because he was doing *Crocodile Dundee 2,* so I did it, got these rave reviews. And all of a sudden he was back and the play wins a Pulitzer Prize and Dutton gets the Tony Award. I'm like, 'That was my shot. That was my shot!'

"Next thing I'm on my knees and broke-down. But you know, it was supposed to happen like that. When it was time for me to hear the message, I heard it. Now it's easy for me not to drink, not to use drugs and do all the stuff that people do to relapse. It's directly correlated to where I am right now. When I was getting high and having a good time, I didn't hear anything. As soon as I stopped, all this happened. So it's kind of like: 'Do you need a drink?' Hell no. 'Do you need some drugs?' Hell no. 'Do you like being rich?' Hell yes. 'You want to be poor and begging people for money and stealing money and lying to people again?' No. So, it isn't a choice. Plus I get to do what I love and I get to choose the things I want to do in the venue that I want to be in.

"Now, folks ask me, 'Why do you work so much?' Well, when I was growing up everybody in my house went to work every day. I didn't grow up with a group of people sitting around waiting for someone to hand them a check. My grandmother worked cleaning up, doing whatever. My grandfather cleaned up those office buildings. My mom worked at a bakery. Everybody went to work. Two weeks of vacation a year, maybe. I thought that's what people did, so in college, I was working in a theater across town. Then, when I got to New York, I started doing theater, and I was always doing a play, auditioning for a play, and rehearsing a play. It was work, work, work because I don't want to wait tables. You know, if you're a waiter, you got to act like a waiter. I knew how to build sets; I knew how to hang lights. I had a degree in theater, so when I got to New York, when I wasn't acting I was building sets.

"In New York, people would ask me, 'Who are you studying with?' I'm like, 'I have a job, I'm an actor.' Even if it's for $35 a week or $35 a month, I'm happy. I'm not paying anybody to do any scenes and sit around and watch anyone else act and criticize. I'm not trying to be a critic. I'm here to act. So I acted wherever I could act. It's just that simple. You go to work. You always go to work. You know what I love about De Niro? He goes to work. Gene Hackman and Michael Caine? They go to work."

However far Sam himself has come, he told me a story that reminded me how far we all still have to go.

"My wife and I got in this car in Scotland when I was over there playing golf at Dunhills," he says. "My daughter is in Edinburgh, just hanging out, pretending to look for a job. We got in this car going to the airport and the guy driving said, 'I'm so glad to be driving you, sir, I now have the full set.'

"I said, 'What are you talking about?'

"He said, 'I've driven Mr. Washington. I've driven the *Shawshank*

Redemption fella.' I said, 'You mean Morgan Freeman?' He said, 'Yes . . . and now I have you. You're the three greatest black actors in America; I now have the full set.'

"I said, 'Get the heck out of here!' "

It really upsets me that one guy—a guy in Scotland, no less—has driven all of the "greatest black actors in America." It's even worse that he could have squeezed them all in the backseat at once.

Samuel L. Jackson, Denzel Washington, and Morgan Freeman made up a "full set"?

Anytime you can name all of them, just like that, you know there's a problem. Now you know damn well those aren't the only great black actors out there. But those are the only guys who get the chance to do a wide variety of roles and show just how great they are.

Samuel L. Jackson, Denzel Washington, Morgan Freeman. You can add Will Smith as well. And that's pretty much the list. That isn't right.

Take Lawrence Fishburne. He's been a great actor for a long time, some twenty-five years. But nobody can really name anything he's been in except the *Matrix* trilogy. And you can't really say those are "his" movies. You think of *The Matrix,* you think of Keanu Reeves, you think of those cool special effects, but Larry doesn't really get the credit for his acting ability. That's unfortunate.

Samuel L. Jackson is on that short list. And I definitely had an appreciation for the way he understands exactly where he is, and what it means.

In that business it's tough for you to get to the mountaintop.

Sports are an anomaly because anyone who's really good can climb the ladder very quickly. In every other profession in this world other than sports, the glass ceiling is there. Even in my profession, all the players are black but the hierarchy is white. But I have great admiration for any black man who does well in anything other than sports, because you'd better be really good.

Sam was really proud of his status as the number one film moneymaker of all time. How many people do you think even know he has that title? He should be proud. After hearing what he had to go through to get there, I know I am.

BUILDING
A CULTURE
OF DIGNITY
PRESIDENT
BILL
CLINTON

Few people move as freely between people of different races as former president Bill Clinton. He has often been called "America's first black president" because of the ease and comfort with which he interacts with black people. The great irony about segregation is that it is often white southerners who are most able to live easily with black folks. In President Clinton's case, it was a feeling that was early translated into action when, at sixteen, he lobbied for a civil rights measure in the platform of his party at the American Legion Boys Nation.

There is clearly an open-mindedness about President Clinton. His office, located in Harlem, has photographs of Ella Fitzgerald, Dizzy Gillespie, Duke Ellington, and Wynton Marsalis on the walls. On the way music bridges racial divides, he was recently quoted as saying, "It's a common language and it speaks to the heart in a place where there's no room for hatred."

I had always wanted to talk to President Clinton. I've always felt a certain connection with him, perhaps because we're both southerners, me from Alabama and him from Arkansas. And while I contend that racism is the greatest cancer of my lifetime, President Clinton long ago called racism "America's constant curse."

So I just felt that any discussion of race in America would be incomplete if I didn't talk . . . well, listen . . . to President Clinton. He was gracious enough to talk to me in his Harlem office one afternoon. And it didn't take long for him to warm to the topic, particularly his own feelings about not tolerating prejudice and about public education, and how its improvement would lead the way in eliminating some of the disparities that affect people daily.

"Well, first of all, look behind you," President Clinton said to me, gesturing to his bookshelves. "If you read all these books, and they're all autobiographies or biographies, there are basically two or three things that they're about. They're about people of uncommon talent who made it against all the odds. They're about people who fought to overcome discrimination directed specifically against them or generally against people of their race. And they're about the continuing problems people have.

"Let's talk first about Americans, and then we ought to talk about the rest of the world, because this is a problem not just in America. If you look at where we are today, it's really interesting because America's got its old problem of race overlaid with this explosion of new immigrants coming into the country—all kinds of colors of people, all kinds of religions, all kinds of backgrounds. In Europe now, they're talking about whether they should reduce immigration, and they're supposed to be more liberal than we are. But I think the number one problem is that even in America we still don't know each other very well. And a lot of white people who know black people, who are friends, think they're the exception to the rule.

"If you look at all the fastest-growing counties in America, most of them are swelling with white middle-class people who really can't afford to move where they're going, but they're looking, they believe, for good schools and safe neighborhoods. Most of the people they're leaving behind are people of color. But there's an increasing number of African Americans who are moving to places like that for the same reasons. That is, they want good schools and safe neighborhoods, too.

"I think there are two or three things that we really need to focus on. One is, we need to know each other better than we do. This whole red state/blue state thing? In Barack Obama's great speech at the Democratic National Convention, he said there are people who live in red states who know gay people they like. That's true, but I look at that and I think again that, in so many cases, we don't know each other. A lot of life is just who you know, and do you really know 'em? We pass people on the street all the time and don't see them. We may even exchange words with people and we don't really talk with them or listen to them. I think that's a huge problem.

"The second thing, I believe, is that we tend to make assumptions about people who aren't in our crowd that aren't accurate. For example, most poor people are not on welfare; they work. I think that most poor people would agree that the best social program is a job and that work is a lot better than welfare. Many, many poor people are the most anticrime people you can imagine, because they're the people most likely to be victimized by it. Most people who live in Harlem really want the same thing for their kids as most people in midtown Manhattan do, or that the Greeks in Queens do. They just don't know how to get it. There's lots of this stuff we just don't even know because we don't talk to each other across racial lines and across income lines and neighborhood lines.

"I think what this country needs as much as anything else right now is a unifying vision of the future that people can buy into—whether they're Republicans, Democrats, conservatives, or liberals—that basically focuses on at least giving everybody a chance to have the life you and I have. You know, you were a great athlete, and I can talk. So we had improbable lives. But we left behind a lot of people who had disappointing lives, who could have done better, if there'd been, I think, a better set of options out there."

I told President Clinton that having been blessed with the life I've had, particularly being black, has put me on a mission lately. While I appreciate my life, I know I'm not the norm. And the gap between rich and poor people seems to be growing so wide. You would think reducing that gap would be people's focus, but it isn't. It's still on the differences between people, even though the differences are often exaggerated and people are more similar than they know.

"I don't think it's very complicated," said President Clinton. "I think we like people who like us. I think most black people have an uncommon sensitivity born of either their own experiences or their parents' or grandparents' experiences. I remember when I was governor, one time I proposed to require that all the teachers in Arkansas had to pass a test to get certified. And it was obvious that more blacks than whites would fail the test because they had a horrible college education, and for that matter a horrible high school education themselves. So I said, 'Take the test as many times as you want to.' I knew that the kids who need good teachers the most will be poor black kids who are never going to have a chance if they don't get an education; without good teachers, they don't have a chance. Well, the teachers union, which was predominantly but not exclusively white, condemned my proposal. So I brought in all these black ministers and I said, 'Look, here's the deal. We're not going to kick anybody out of the classroom who's a good person who's been there for years because they fail this test one time. But they've got to be able to know their stuff to really be right for the kids. We'll give them two years.' So the black ministers endorsed my program, which totally undercut the opposition, and it passed.

"Sure enough, it worked just about like I thought it would. At first there was a higher failure rate for black teachers, but then, after two years, the pass rate almost evened up. But the black community never would have agreed to it if they hadn't believed that I believed in their future and I was on their side.

"I don't think it's very complicated. I just think it's partly a matter of the heart: People feel you're with them or not."

People of all races and nationalities seem to feel comfortable around President Clinton. And there seems to be an awareness and openness in him that people connect with. I had always wondered, since I first became aware of him as governor of Arkansas, how he developed his philosophy of compassion and equality.

"I deserve no credit for it," President Clinton insisted. "I was lucky. I was raised to a significant extent by my grandparents. Even after my mother remarried, I spent a lot of time with my grandparents. My grandfather had a sixth-grade education and ran a country store in a black neighborhood in a rural town in Arkansas. When black people came in without any money, he gave them food on credit if he thought they were working and doing the best they could. And he had me play with black kids when I was four years old, right behind the grocery store. He thought the whole thing of segregation was wrong. The Central High School crisis was the year he died, but before that whole thing ever happened, he was for integrating the schools. His wife—my grandmother—was a nurse. She had a correspondence degree from the Chicago School of Nursing, and she was pro–civil rights. I don't know why they were. Most white people who were lower middle class weren't; they needed somebody to look down on. For some reason my grandparents didn't.

"So I just all my life felt that way because I was taught that way, which was highly unusual for a white kid growing up in rural Arkansas in the forties and fifties, early sixties. I never could figure out why anybody should look down on anybody else because they were different. I always found it exciting to be around different people. I'd rather be around all kinds of folks, and not just different by the color of their skin. I like being around people of different religions, people who have different politics. I never felt the need to look down on anybody. I was raised that way, and my mother was that way. My mother was less political than her parents, but she was a nurse—an anesthetist. She put people to sleep for surgery. She'd say, 'I don't see how anybody could be a racist who ever operated on people. Once you watch people bleed, it's all the same.'

"It wasn't sophisticated, it wasn't. It was just pure gut. That's the way my family was, and I inherited it. I deserve no credit for it."

Like President Clinton, I'm really concerned about not just black kids, but poor people in general in this country. It seems the best chance they have of succeeding is by getting a good education. But the public school system in this country is hurting. I've wondered about some of the possible solutions.

"It's an issue I've been working on for twenty-five years," President Clinton said. "When my family moved to Washington, we put our daughter in a private school, but mostly it was for privacy reasons. Before that she went to a public junior high school where a majority of kids were black and a majority of kids were poor, and where several of the girls she went to school with had already had babies. It was the best thing that ever happened to her. But they also had good teachers and the kids that went there got a pretty good education.

"Let me say that nearly every problem in American public education has been solved by somebody somewhere. The thing with public education—and this is what we ought to think about—is that, unlike basketball, unlike politics, you can copy somebody who's doing it better than you are. If you're out there playing basketball and somebody's beating you every night, every time you play them, and you want to win, you got to figure out what they're doing and how to do it better. The same thing in politics."

As President Clinton is talking, I see what he means. In sports, in politics, you're trying to beat an opponent; there's only one winner and one loser. But in education, all schools can win. And they can im-

prove by looking at those that are succeeding and using them as models.

"I'll give you this one example," he continued. "Less than a mile from here there's a New York City public school called Frederick Douglass Academy. It's nearly a hundred percent black. It's a public school—choice school, that is. You have to ask to go there, but there's no screening for income, IQ, nothing. The only thing you have to do is agree to abide by the uniform policy, and the parents have to agree to show up when they're asked. And that's it. When I went there two years ago, about ninety-eight percent of the kids graduated. Over ninety percent went on to some form of higher education. And their test scores were above the New York State average. These are poor black kids in New York City. They've been sponsored by The Gap and HBO. There's a store in the school that sells uniforms, and the kids get to work in the store and earn money. Their families can buy the clothes that their kids need at cost. For the rest of the family, they can buy sweaters and stuff like that. You can go in there tomorrow and it's spic-and-span clean. We wouldn't have to announce that Charles Barkley and Bill Clinton are showing up. We just show up at the front door, we could sit down on the floor and eat breakfast. They've created a culture.

"Now, how come within three miles of this there are other high schools that aren't that good? That's the question that we have to answer. What can the federal government do? What can the states do? What does the local school district have to do?

"I don't want to oversimplify this, but I've seen schools like this in Chicago. I've seen schools like this in Washington, D.C. There was a junior high school in Washington, D.C.—Thomas Jefferson Junior

High School—that opened when Ulysses Grant was president. It was ninety-six percent African American. They had a woman from south Louisiana as principal, African American woman. She was six feet tall. They had all these retired black professionals from the Gold Coast it's called—the longtime affluent black neighborhood in northwest Washington—come in and teach. And that school sent a team to the national junior high school mathematics final. Three out of four years in the mid-1980s, they were one of the four best schools in the whole country. They had a maintenance man who'd been there thirty years, and it was the cleanest building I've ever been in in my life. It looked like it had opened last year. Again, the point I want to make is that we have to learn how to replicate excellence if we want these schools to work.

"I think some competition is good; that's why I favor these public school choice plans. The problem with the voucher system—letting people take the money and go to a private school—is it's never enough to cover the cost and you may take more away from the public school than you give to the kids in the private school. Now, the No Child Left Behind Act, which nearly everybody supported, the Democrats and President Bush and everybody, hasn't been adequately funded. But it's a start. What it says is every state has to pick a certain set of tests, and if the kids don't do well on them, then the school has to improve. I favor a slightly different system, but I think what the federal government ought to do is to create incentives for schools to replicate those that work. North Carolina had the biggest improvement of student scores of any state in the country when I was president. And basically, they had a system that says, if a school is failing, they'll give it two years to turn around, and if not, they're going to shut it down and put it under new management. The key to this is normally the principal. In some big cities, the key is being able to have the flexibility to change principals, and then giving the principal the authority to run the school. That's why Chicago is doing better since they put the control under the mayor.

"Of course, you have to look at every state and every school district, and what needs to be done in each would be slightly different. But if all these poor black kids in the Frederick Douglass Academy can score higher than the New York State average and go on to college, there is no excuse for not figuring out how to do this repeatedly. Remember: There's no screening for IQ. There's no screening for income. There's no screening for anything. They created a culture that people wanted to be a part of.

"The point I want to make is that you can do it. I had a friend named Ollie McEnmoore, who was an African American woman from the Mississippi Delta in Arkansas. She came from this county up on the river, one of the poorest counties in America. So I'm running for president in 1992 and I was in Chicago and I said, 'Tell me where there's a good school.' So I go to this school, Ollie McEnmoore is the principal, and it's a junior high school in the highest crime area in Chicago. I go in and there's a uniform policy, there's a no-tolerance-for-weapons policy: One knife found in your locker and you're gone. Again, you had to request to get in, but there's no income, no IQ, no grade requirement. But the parents have to be willing to show up and the kids have to follow the school uniform policy. Every week, they had 150 mothers and 75 fathers show up in that school to help. The kids scored way above the Illinois average on the test scores. They had a zero dropout rate. They were the happiest kids I ever saw. Those kids that have miserable situations at home felt they were safe in school. They felt like they were important; they felt like they could be somebody. You know, I think that's the thing that's been lost in a lot of this public school debate, when people argue about vouchers or anything else. We have to ask ourselves the simple question: When there are these unbelievably successful schools out there and the children enrolled in them are not rich or from more stable families or have higher IQs than the kids stuck in all these bad schools, how come all the bad schools don't become more like the good schools?

"Basically, the deal is, you've got to get a good principal who is well trained and understands that he or she has to create a culture. Kids have to feel like they're on a team. They all have to feel like they're somebody and they can make something of themselves. Whatever the barriers are to running those schools—and there will be some at the local, state, and national levels—they've got to be cleared away. The incentive structure needs to be set up. They'll get better and better.

"Everybody can do something. There's a billionaire named Eli Broad, out in California, who set up a foundation. His whole mission now, having retired from his business, is to get good people from the military, from business, from wherever to come in, train them to be principals and then go out and place them."

President Clinton also made it clear that, even though education is a system where all schools can win, it's healthy for there to be some competition among them.

"For all of our public school problems," he said, "everybody concedes we've got the best system of higher education in the world. There are hundreds of colleges, of all sizes, where you can get a world-class undergraduate education. Some are private, some are public, but they can't stay in business if they don't give you something good. So in precollege education, there has to be some competition. That's the argument of all the people who say the answer is to give every parent a voucher and let them take it to the public schools or the private schools, wherever they want. The problem with that argument is, in general, a lot of these schools are underfunded. So you might help five kids with the vouchers but hurt fifty kids for the same amount of money who could have had a better education otherwise. The other thing is, not all the private schools perform markedly better than the public ones. The best ones do, and that's why people go to them. But we have to talk about it nationally. Why are the great public schools not being copied or emulated?

"Let me just say one other thing. When you and I die, there will still be social problems in America, in our world. If you've got bad government policy and a weak economy, and nobody's helping people get a job and the schools aren't good, I think you ought to think, if nothing goes the way you think it should, what can you say about why you turned out the way you did?

"I used to watch you—you know, this is the first time we've ever talked—I used to watch you all the time play basketball, and I thought: How come this guy who can't jump very high gets all these rebounds from these guys who are six inches taller? And then when you got older and you couldn't run very fast, I watched you use your body to get in a position to make shots. And I thought, 'What's going through his head that makes all these young fast kids not be able to defeat him?' All great contests in life are head games. You get two people with more or less equal physical abilities, and they both work hard and shoot free throws; it's the one with the better head who's going to win.

"You need to leave people reading your book with a message. Suppose none of this stuff I want to happen in education actually happens. Suppose there are racists out there confronting me. Suppose there are terrible government policies in place and you aren't getting the help you need. Suppose some schools are good and some are lousy. What can you put in their heads, kids and adults, that will increase their chances to be what they ought to be? Life itself is like all great contests; it's a series of head games. You know, running for president's a head game. They try to take you down. They try to tell you how bad you are; they try to derail you. What they're really trying to do is not turn the voters off of you; they're trying to turn *you* off of you. They try to get you where your head doesn't work anymore. And you spend all your time answering all your critics and basically feeling terrible about yourself and everything else. It's a head game.

"You ought to make sure you impress upon anybody reading your book that if none of this stuff works out, if you're a poor black kid or you're a poor Latino kid, you've had a rough life, you've got a terrible home life, your school isn't worth a damn, nobody cared about you, here's what you ought to think about . . ."

President Clinton didn't finish that sentence, but he'd made the point perfectly clear. Everything in the world might be against you. But like those kids who entered those schools he talked about who didn't have the highest IQ or family income, it's still possible to succeed through sheer effort, discipline, and education. When he was talking about those kids going to school and wearing uniforms

every day, he was emphasizing that dignity doesn't come through trendy clothes and bling-bling. You can get ahead despite your circumstances—white or black—by going to school, by doing whatever you can to get the best education possible.

It seemed perfectly appropriate that one of the rare folks who moves comfortably among people of all races had focused our conversation primarily on a goal on which most people, white and black, would agree.

COLOR
TELEVISION
GEORGE
LOPEZ

Sandra Bullock once said of George Lopez, "I fell in love with George's life story. He has a personal history like a train wreck and he's brave enough to share it. He speaks the truth and opens people's minds in other directions."

So you know right off the bat why I wanted to talk with George, because he's had such a difficult journey to the top, because he is the co-creator, writer, producer, and star of the ABC sitcom "George Lopez." Because he was abandoned by his migrant-worker father at two months old and his mother ten years later. Because he was inspired by comedians Freddie Prinze Sr. and Richard Pryor. Because he fought through alcohol and depression. And yes, because he is

Chicano and oftentimes is a loud and brutally persuasive voice on concerns of Hispanics in America.

There are a whole lot of reasons to listen to George, whether he's engaged or in a comedic rant. But when we talked with him, I wanted to start with his show and how rare it is for a Chicano to be in control—to some degree—over the content, the cast and crew, and the portrayal of a family of color on network television.

"It's a situation," George said, "where I'm the executive producer, where it's my show . . . but is it my show? We wouldn't be here if it wasn't for George Lopez. And yet, if I'm unhappy with the performance of some people on the show, do I have the power to replace them? I'd like to think I do because it's my place and all these people who are on the show are from my life. But I couldn't create a show without the studio and without the network. So at what point do they say, 'Now it's a product.' It's still my life. That's still the lady who plays my mother. That's still the lady who plays my wife. Their names are almost the same as my family members. It's a portrayal of me. The perception is of me. I can't just be happy to be here."

He wasn't an ideal candidate to be in this position a few years ago. To quote from *Why You Crying*, George's 2004 autobiography, "I'm as tragic as anyone out there, maybe a little more so." He elaborated.

"Five years ago I was as dead as any performer could be . . . well, other than that I had some signs of life from my work as a comedian. What comedians never want to become is a road comedian—when all your money is made on the road. I had a wife and a daughter, and I always aspired to be more than that. I always thought I could be more than that. But what I had become was a road comedian, because I couldn't get an audition because nobody was hiring Latinos. If there's a buddy movie they go black and white. Commercials, they could have a million faces and not one Latino. Literally, you could look at a Honda commercial where there were a hundred faces and there wasn't one Latino. But if you looked at Telemundo, they'd have a Honda commercial with all Mexicans in it. You know, like you had to buy a Mexican Honda. Nothing is more American than McDonald's, but you'll see a white McDonald's commercial with only white patrons, and then the same commercial but with black patrons . . . but not together.

"I thought, 'Here I am, this is what I've got to say, and I'm either going to hit it out of the park or I'm going to just be a road comedian.' No one got it in the eighties when I was doing it, I'd get pulled off the stage, man. I'd get pulled off. I'd talk about my grandmother, I'd talk about curing ailments with ginger ale and 7-Up, about killing the chicken in the yard, about birthday parties that had more beer than kids, you know—all the stuff that I saw. I said, 'Hey, that's my thing.' I have to talk about what makes us who we are, you know? There is funny stuff all over the place, but when I tried to take ours to a larger scale, very few people wanted to hear it."

But George wanted to tell these stories from his life because he felt, as do many Hispanics, that their individual stories just get left out of American storytelling, even though they're becoming the largest minority group in the United States. George was worried that the perception of who he was would prevent him from having the chance to tell his story. He knows there's a certain me-versus-the-world mentality that he wears on his sleeve because, he admits, "I grew up angry, alone, teased, and tormented. I grew up around nobodies as a nobody wanting to be something else."

So the chip on his shoulder was necessary to get through adolescence but not everybody knows or understands why he has it or what it means.

"You know, if I smile I can disarm anybody," George said. "But when I don't smile people are afraid. They don't know what's going on. They think I'm in a bad mood. 'Cause I'm an only child so I internalize everything. You know, I don't say to people, 'Excuse me, let me ask your opinion.' I got ridges on my forehead because I sit quietly and watch and think. I spent so much time that way as a kid. I think everything I think is inside. So people would think, you know, 'He's moody.' Man, I was the biggest teddy bear in the world. I loved people. Today I'm giving this guy $700 to give to a fifteen-year-old foster kid so she can have a *quincenera,* because she doesn't have the money to do it. I just feel that a kid should have a party when they turn fifteen. I didn't, but you know, a kid should have those moments where they invite their friends.

"I'm going to be the one that's going to break through when no one else could. Paul Rodriguez couldn't do it, couldn't take it to the level at which it's sustainable. Freddie Prinze killed himself trying. Desi Arnaz did it but that was fifty years ago and he drank himself literally to death. So the legacy, the history of Latino performers, wasn't one filled with, well, positivity.

"I'd come from nowhere, I'm dark-skinned, and I hated it when I was a little kid. I look like I'm Indian. People don't know if I'm Native American, if I'm Mexican. Mexicans will claim me now because

I'm doing well. But people don't know what I am. Dark skin fright-
ens people. Dark scares anybody. Just the thought of it scares some
people. I called a restaurant, told the person on the phone, 'I'd like
to make reservations for my wife and me.' So we're chatting. I'm making the girl laugh and she says, 'Your name?' I say, 'Lopez.' And
there's silence. She says, 'Wow, you don't sound Hispanic.' I said,
'What the hell?' That goes to the vein. So I tried to make a joke and
said, 'You didn't sound stupid till you said that.' Everything that happens to me, instead of getting angry, I try to turn it to a joke. So it's
like a tractor going through a field picking up all this crap and turning it into something good. My theory now is go where they don't
want you to go. That's my theory now."

**It's interesting to see George alternate between annoyed and some-
times angry and laughing. What he knows, because he produces and
writes for his own sitcom, is how important perception is and how difficult it is if the people writing and producing have no idea what your
life is like. That's one of the recurring themes in the conversations we
had for this book, whether it was Ice Cube or Peter Guber or George
making the observation. Perception really becomes reality if you
aren't careful. And too many times the people creating the perception
don't have any sense of your reality.**

"Most of the people who live in Hollywood, who are decision-
making people, don't live in less than absolute affluence or opu-
lence," George said. "And many of them never have known otherwise.
They take the money and they go and live in huge places. This is a
great example. They asked me to do the Emmy preshow; it was at this
dude's house in Bel Air. So the car takes me to Bel Air . . . it's a beau-

tiful house. I'm already thinking, when I arrive, about how people who live like this and write these shows see Latinos and blacks as a subculture that exists to provide the help. Anyway, walking up to the house, I see a Latina walking three dogs. I see Latinas pushing the carriage. So my first thought is 'modern-day slavery.' Then I'm reasoning that these women have to work. Yet you know they're probably not being paid much more than minimum wage . . . maybe the minimum. Anyway, I go to the house. The lady who answers the door is a Latina lady in a uniform, in a damn maid's uniform. So I told my wife—my wife's Cuban—and she said, 'Why is she wearing a uniform?' and I said, 'Oh, I don't know, so they won't confuse her as being part of the family?' Because it's a form of suppression, man, and when the dude writes a script or treatment, he doesn't see us as being anything else.

"People talk about bigotry as if it's a thing of the past, like it's some museum exhibit. It's here, man. It's right now. When rich people are in the car, they lock the doors. They lock the windows. They have a certain way they drive. And they never go another way. So they never see. When they go to baseball games, they have good seats; they never really get in contact with those who are different from them. That's why, when they go to donate clothes, it's a big thing for them. You know, when they clean out their closets and have a yard sale.

"This guy who's a jeweler told me a great story. He'd left his jewels on top of the car one day . . . a big bag of jewels. They fell off. He gets to the office and he couldn't find them and he went nuts. There's hundreds of thousands of dollars' worth of jewels in this bag he can't find. When he gets home, he's just torn up: 'Oh God, I lost a whole bag of jewels!' And the housekeeper has them. She found them in the driveway—she brought them inside—and she gave them to him, and he's like, 'George, she could not have been more honest.' It's, like, a shock to him. He couldn't believe she was capable of being honest. His expectation was that she'd keep them, and he couldn't comprehend that she'd possess manners or honesty or dignity.

"I think so much of this has to do with the way we're portrayed in the movies, on TV. It's how writers see people of color. And this is the only contact a lot of people in this country have with Hispanics or blacks. I used to play golf with these dudes and one day one of the dudes said to me—I swear to God, true story—'I've got to ask you some questions after we're done playing; I'm working on a project.' I said, 'All right.' I was thinking he must have some comedy-related questions. He said, 'Now, with maids and people like that, where would they live?' I said, 'What in the world are you talking about?' He said, 'Would they take the bus? My maid has a car, but in general do they have buses that they take or what?' He was writing this show about maids, a sitcom. And I said, 'Jimmy, nobody wants to see that shit.'

"One of the things that I never wanted to do with my show was make the characters sitcommie-type people where—and this is the number one thing—the parents are trying to be friends with their kids. You know, in my house, I'm not trying to be a friend to my daughter. I love my daughter, but I want to teach her that there are consequences if you do something that's wrong. It's the same thing with these kids in the show. Now, in other families, the parents are trying to be friends with the kids, go back and forth with them like the kids are adults, give them adult alternatives. I didn't have alternatives when I was growing up. I want my kid to know, 'If I do this, there are consequences that are coming my way.' I was somewhere recently when I saw this lady begging her kid, asking him, 'Do you want to see

Harry Potter or do you want to see your grandmother?' The kid said, 'I want to go see *Harry Potter.*' Of course, he wanted to see *Harry Potter.* I would have told him, 'We're going to grandma's house and if you don't behave yourself, you're not going to go see *Harry Potter.*' And that's what I tried to bring to the show, the concept that I grew up another way, a way I don't see from white families in mainstream TV; we battle with kids, especially when they're teenagers, because they think they know everything.

"Another thing is that we're never going to be criminal on this show. My son vandalizes; any kid could do that. But we're not having a kid on this show who winds up dealing or getting into drugs. My wife's not going to become a maid or take in wash to make ends meet, you know? We're going to struggle like any family would struggle, but we're not having a show that gives into all those damn stereotypes that we've seen Latinos put in all these years. We're not having that."

It's rare for a guy involved with a show to be that emotionally invested in the show in that particular way. But George is as invested in "George Lopez" as Bill Cosby was with "The Cosby Show" when it debuted on NBC twenty years ago. The big problem is the characters in shows featuring people of color don't have any range, usually. Too often, the characters of color are childlike or overly comedic. Black writers in Hollywood are even rarer than prime-time dramas featuring black characters. I watch a whole lot of television and I see a whole lot of movies. There are days when I'll watch several movies a day, a lot of good ones, too. And there are plenty of cases where characters could be black or Hispanic or Asian, but rarely are. Those "Friends" in New York City couldn't have one black friend, or Asian friend, or Hispanic friend? Like that doesn't happen in New York. I

don't know what's worse: not having nonwhite characters or not having nonwhite writers who understand what to do with the characters.

"The problem with all the Latino shows, like 'AKA Pablo' twenty years ago," George said, "is that there always seemed to be about thirteen kids in the house. Norman Lear did it, very stereotypical. 'Viva Valdez' was about a family that won the lottery and moved to Bel Air. It was short-lived. My show was going to be about a guy who had a mother who still thought he was ten and a wife who wants him to be a better husband and a father to these children when he didn't have a father. There was nothing in it about being Mexican. I told the writers, 'Bring me stories and bring me jokes and don't worry about writing Latino.' Because the Latino writers we tried to get, they were so focused on Mexican stuff, the show wouldn't have succeeded. Nobody would have watched had it gone that 1970s route. Even they had bought into the stereotype, which is tough because you think the only way you can make it is to give in to the system, which is, 'We gotta write *Boys 'N the Hood*. After *Boys 'N the Hood* there were tons of them, right? But there's only one groundbreaking one. After that, it's mostly just being a gangster and black exploitation junk. You narrow your own selves to try to sell stuff instead of saying, 'I'm going to write human conditions and human situations.' That's what I wanted—I wanted human situations. And I was going to be the color that would paint the show. The industry is compartmentalized to do that, to say 'Soul Food' could only be on Showtime. But it, or some show like it, couldn't be on CBS? That doesn't make any sense to me. They look at it and just automatically say, 'Let's put it on cable.' It's a great show. 'Resurrection Blvd.' was on Showtime and somehow the love was thrown to one show, but not the other. And 'Resurrection Blvd.' ended up going away instead of staying; it could have been a great two hours of programming. I don't think it should be so hard to produce dramatic programming featuring people of color. What's so hard about it? And I think audiences of all colors would watch. I think we can be dramatic. I think you see that with Taye Diggs's show.

"Look at Whoopi Goldberg. I mean Whoopi Goldberg's a huge star. She won an Academy Award for best supporting actress in *Ghost,* and she had to beg to get the back nine. That tells you that even an Academy Award–winning actress had to go in there and plead her case for her show to continue at least through the season. In terms of production and writing, it's better than when I started, but it's not like the floodgates are going to open. It's going to come through process, man, through time.

"When I came to the stage to see Nikki Cox when she had a show, I saw the set and the crew were all white. And Sandra Bullock, who's my executive producer, came over and said, 'Why are there only white people?' And she said, 'Well, it isn't going to be like that when we do our show.' So when we film, we now have a Mexican sound dude, a Mexican boom operator, white female camera operator, Asian prop guy, Mexican prop guy, Latino camera director. It's a mix because my obligation is not to beat them over the head but to let them know that I know how to be inclusive. I know what's going on. You can't overthrow the government in a day. It takes time. But if you proceed forward and always do things from the heart and things that are good for other people instead of just going off and just shutting everything down, I think things get better."

I don't accept the notion that white people won't watch shows featuring black people. What the hell was "The Cosby Show"? It was

number three in the Nielsen ratings when it first came on in 1984, and then it was the number one show in 1985, 1986, 1987, 1988, and 1989. It was never out of the top twenty in eight years. There aren't enough black people in America to make a show number one in the Nielsen ratings, especially since I don't even know if any black people have a Nielsen box in their house. Seriously, I've never met a black person in my life who lived in a Nielsen family. Never seen one. I asked Mike Wilbon and he doesn't know any black person who has ever had a Nielsen box either. So when you take that factor, and look at how popular "The Cosby Show" was and "Sanford and Son," you have to think that TV executives are either dead wrong or lying if they think shows with black families can't attract white viewers or appeal to advertisers.

"Hey, man, what Mexican or black person is going to let you put a box in their house when they don't know what the hell it is?" George said, cracking up, when I mentioned this. "You know, our people, man, might call somebody and say, 'Get that box out of my house! It's probably a camera somebody is installing in here to watch us!' But seriously, there is a guy named Alex Nogales, with the National Hispanic Media Coalition, who has been lobbying to get the percentage of Latino Nielsen families increased to 13 percent, which would reflect the percentage of Latinos in the country, up from 7 percent where it has been. And blacks are also underrepresented. It's an antiquated system in which people who comprise nearly one quarter of all the people in the country are barely counted. And we're talking about the damn medium that might be the most important thing in popular culture. It reminds you of what an exclusive club the networks and the big cable companies are. The big white executives, the moment one is fired, it's like, 'Hey, come on over to "ER." We'll make room for you here.' They regenerate themselves. You know what happens to us? When we premiered, Bernie Mac and Cedric the Entertainer—two incredibly talented dudes—were moved against Damon Wayans and me, head to head. Fox did that purposely. And Bernie's show lost steam and Cedric's got canceled after six weeks.

"It's difficult for any show, when they move you around. For the people who program, their priority is not people of color on TV. Their priority is, 'Where am I gonna get the next "Friends" ' or 'Where am I going to get the next "Two and a Half Men," ' you know? The fact is, if you put anyone behind 'Everybody Loves Raymond,' that show is going to be huge. Now, when Raymond leaves, what's going to hold up comedies? One good point could be that Damon Wayans and I have done well together, and now the focus could shift over to NBC because they've got a black and Latino guy for the first time since 'Sanford and Son' and 'Chico and the Man' in 1973.

"The WB built its network on the strength of black viewers," George said. "But as soon as the network got successful from that strategy working, they canceled all the shows targeting black viewers and put on '7th Heaven' and 'Smallville.' But they built the network with black shows. This is a prime example of how Hollywood operates. They use the Wayans brothers and Robert Townsend, their talent, to build the network. Yeah, it's an opportunity to create a show. And those guys took advantage of it and built shows that allowed the network to become solid. They build the WB network on the backs of black shows. Strong shows, strong performers and performances. Then, as the foundation settles, they figure, 'We're solid now. Now we can cut back on "those" shows,' which of course means the black shows, and then they bring in the white shows. I guess it's kind of like parts of America . . . built black, went white. I'm not saying you shouldn't have a mix of shows on any network, because that's what they ought to have. That's what they ought to be striving for. And the Wayans brothers are brilliant—I thought *White Chicks* was very funny. But when you take away the only place where black shows can air, it makes it harder for young African American writers, producers, and stars to get a show on WB, because suddenly they're not doing that anymore, even though that's how they became a successful network in the first place."

It seems like there is quite a bit of pressure on George Lopez. He's very aware of his own life early on and the pressures of the TV business, particularly on women and people of color.

"We're sixty-three shows in," George says, "and what I learned in the sixty-three weeks that I've been here is that we have an inherent genetic system built in to destroy ourselves through whatever it is, through alcohol, through womanizing, through drinking and driving. There are elements inside of us that we have to control every day: rage, anger, disrespect. I go through those things every day but I know that what I've created so far is good, that I'm not going to destroy it. Roseanne went nuts. Brett Butler on 'Grace Under Fire' went nuts. You go nuts because you don't know how to play the game. This is all a game. This was somebody else's trailer, and when I leave, all my pictures will be gone. This will become the next person's trailer. But the game is on right now, so to stay in the game you can't blow up, blow out or else you're out of the game. You can't say 'I'm hurt.' You have to stay in the game. So what I've learned is instead of taking people to task and freaking out, let's see if we can work it out in a mild manner, which is totally against my personality. But I'm think-

ing all that for the good of the woman who plays my wife who struggled for twenty years, for the woman who plays my mother who was
retired and was an acting coach, for the guy who plays my best friend
who started acting on dirt stages in Texas. And I'm thinking about all
this because of my obligation as George Lopez and as the dude who
grew up an only child raised by his grandparents, who saw Freddie
Prinze in 1973 and said, 'That's what I want to be. . . . What I want
to be is a comedian.' If I destroy myself, then what have I done for
my people?

"What I can leave them, hopefully, is a show that will run forever
and ever. My wife walks over at Fryman Canyon all the time. And
there's a lady over there, a domestic, who says when I walk with my
wife, 'Oh my God if my son was here he would trip out. He's a huge
fan of yours and he said, "Because of George Lopez, Mom, maybe I
can be on TV." ' And when you hear those things . . . that's why you
don't go nuts.

"You know what I tell kids . . . all kids? Forget about dreaming; instead set goals. Dreams are: I want to go to the moon. It may not happen. But if you say, 'I want to grow up and be a comedian' or 'I want
to grow up and be a doctor' or 'I want to be the first one to graduate
from high school in my family,' which I was, all that is possible and
race has no deterrent in that, in the outcome."

**While George's show may be about the life of a Chicano in Amer-
ica, the humor works because it's about a family. Anybody can relate
to the problems in the Lopez TV household or the Huxtable TV
household. George, like Bill Cosby before him, knew a lot of ugliness
before he got to know what a traditional family looked like and felt
like. Remember, as George writes in his autobiography, his dad left**

the family when he was two months old and his mother left when he was ten. Luckily for him, he had a great extended family, but no family could protect him from the realities of racial prejudice.

"When I was thirteen," he said of his first experience learning about race, "we started going to these bike races, and this guy was calling me Pedro. He just kept calling me Pedro. 'Hey Pedro.' And I was thinking, why is this guy calling me Pedro? What the hell is he talking about? So I asked my friend's dad about it and he went completely nuts because he knew what was going on. And it finally dawns on me what is happening and I'm thinking, 'Is that what this is?' I'm a kid. I didn't know. I didn't know it was like somebody calling me a 'Beaner.' Hey, I'm the darkest person in my family; as I said in my book, 'I don't even think I'm related to everybody else in my family.' I said, 'I think my mom was with somebody else.' That's what I think, right? When you see my family and you see me with them, you start thinking they're like the Munsters. There's the blond girl and the rest of them are the Munsters? You're looking at this one kid who looks different and you're wondering, 'Who is that person?' Nobody in my family had ever done anything. Nobody had graduated from high school. Nobody had done much of anything. They were just takers. All takers, and I'm a giver. We had a lemon tree in the backyard. In the summer I would get so dark I would be called nigger, and black nigger. They would say, 'Why are you so dark? Did your mom sleep with a black dude?' And I would take the lemons and rub them on my arms to try to lighten my skin.

"Of course, as I sit here with you right now, I would not change one line, one scar, one level of pigment in my skin because this is the container that makes the biggest difference, not Antonio Banderas and

Andy Garcia—whom I love—with fair skin. When you look Hispanic and you're in America and you lead your own sitcom, which has never been done successfully, that's when you start to change things."

Sometimes, when I'm frustrated and thinking about some of this stuff, about how conscious an effort blacks and Latinos have to make to hire people of color and why it's important, my wife will say, "Damn, honey, you sound like Farrakhan." And I tell her, "No, I'm not Farrakhan, but white people don't need to think about race." I told my agent the same thing. He said, "You think I'm a racist?" And I said, "Absolutely not. But when you needed to hire somebody, you hired your son, then your other son. And I understand that completely. But I've been with you for fifteen years and you've never hired a black person." I told him that black people don't have the luxury of not thinking about race, but white people do. It doesn't affect them 99 percent of the time. They've got not only the access to money, but the access to power and authority. It's sure as hell not like anybody white with means ever has to go to a black person or to a Latino to ask for anything . . . like a job or a loan. As much money as I may have, I still have to go and ask a white guy for a job. That's just the way it is. If I'm going to work at Turner Sports, that's just the way it is. Or any other network. That's why, while I'm in a position to have some leverage—I call it the hammer—I have to use it to try and help bring in some people who might not get a chance otherwise. I'm not going to always have that leverage.

"I talk to Carlos Santana a lot," George said, "and as tranquil as he seems, he's tormented inside by injustice and by insensitivity. And when he does say something, it's perceived as anger and people shut down. He told me on the phone, 'Man, you got such a gift because you can say what you say and people laugh and they get the message but they get to laugh, too.'

"I went to this huge benefit—we probably raised $5 million—huge thing, Leonardo DiCaprio, president of MGM, billionaires, and they asked me to host it. On every table was my comedy CD. And I noticed that people had left it. I could see that nobody had even picked it up. So I said, 'Hey, that's my CD on the table, my comedy CD, and if you don't want it, give it to the people who work for you, I'm sure they want it.' There's this uncomfortable moment, and I said, 'You mean to tell me in this room right here, none of you guys have Latinos who come and work for you?' Now it's really quiet, and I said, 'None of you have ever built a fence and hired Mexicans to do it?' I said, 'I live where you live. I see what you see. I live in your neighborhood.' Now they started to clap. I said, 'You can't bullshit me, I live amongst you.' My wife is Cuban, and this roofer we had is white. He's coming to sell me a $28,000 composite shingle roof. We're standing there: me, my wife, and the roofer. And this lady comes along, walking her dog, and she says, 'I'm so happy you guys bought the house, it's such a nice house, it just needs the roof.' She's looking at my wife and the roofer. My wife says, 'Oh no, this is my husband. He's the roofer.' That lady took her dog and left. The next day, there was a cake at the house with a note that said, 'My apologies.' I told my wife, 'That bitch is gonna have to bring over more than a cake. It's going to cost her more than a cake.'

"In my everyday life I have no trouble with African American people. I have no trouble with white people—although I kinda do," he said with a chuckle. "I have no trouble with Latinos, although I think we could be farther ahead and do more for ourselves every day. There's ignorance in all people. Ignorance is my enemy. It's the ignorance from assumption, from lifestyle, from the presumptions. . . . Like when somebody comes up to me and says, 'You know, I have a cousin that's married to a Mexican person.' "

People will say something as stupid as that just because they're looking for some bond, any connection they can find. But ignorance is a hard barrier to overcome.

I think most white people who don't like black people simply haven't been around black people. They go by the perception of what somebody said on television or what's portrayed in the media. People always tell me, "I didn't like you." First of all, they'd never met me before. They were judging me based on something they'd heard.

Some people don't like me just because I'm famous and their life sucks. I try not to take it personally. I hope people like me. But if they don't I don't take it personally. They bring their preconceived notions. If they like me, they like me. If they don't, I have to prove myself. But I'll never change my personality for anyone. I just try to be consistent.

I know who I am. More than anything else, I'm lucky. If I wasn't a great basketball player, I'd be stuck in Leeds, Alabama. You have to be fortunate to escape poverty. It's more than just work; there are a lot of hardworking people just spinning their wheels, going nowhere.

I do know that I appreciate my life more now, and I appreciate the people who are less fortunate than I am, because I've been on both ends of the spectrum.

The funny thing about being rich is that people will do all kinds of things for you they'd never consider doing for poor people. That trips me out. People buy me drinks all the time, even though I have

more money than they do. But they didn't want to buy me anything when my family was on welfare.

I like to joke that it's the secret to how rich people stay rich: They get so much free stuff. I get free golf clubs, golf balls, golf bags . . . if I was poor, they wouldn't send me that.

George Lopez enjoys all the perks that come with fame and money—especially when he thinks back to how his life began.

"I love that I grew up poor," he said, "and didn't realize how little money we had until one time when I was in my twenties and I saw an old bank book that my grandfather had. We were worse off than I thought. We had no money, none. We were living week to week, I didn't know that. I mean, there was always heat. Now, I have a great wife, I have a great kid. I love golf. I have great cars. I don't have to apologize for being successful while a lot of blacks and a lot of Latinos feel they have to. If Donald Trump buys a yacht, he's throwing a party and he's showing everyone the yacht. But Oscar de la Hoya moved out of East L.A. to the Hollywood Hills and he's a punk, a sellout. What is that? I mean, nothing against East Los Angeles, but if you had your choice, where would you be? So when Hammer sold his likeness to the British Knights, the shoe company, they started doing commercials, Hammer for British Knights. A ton of black people said, 'Hammer was a punk. He sold out.' Now everybody does it. How come the first brother to do it was a punk sellout?

"Let me tell you something. Oscar is going through stuff I will never have to go through. Instead of being happy for this guy when he won a gold medal for his mom, he's called a punk. Because of all the broken dreams and the fractured aspirations that everybody in that neighborhood had, they turn on one dude because he got out?

They're not happy for him and they should be happy for him. My phone doesn't ring to say, 'I saw you at the Emmys' or 'I saw you on Jimmy Kimmel' or 'Congratulations on your third place in the AT&T celebrity golf tournament.' But if I get canceled, that sucker will ring off the hook. And that's where we live and I know that, so what inspires me is the search for continued success.

"Richard Pryor used to say, 'Be happy for any person doing well.' It sounds simple, but it's hard. When I was struggling, I used to hate people who did well. I started seriously thinking, 'Why do I hate that this dude got a show? Because I don't have a show? Why don't I have a show? I'll go get a show.' When you start to think, 'I'll be happy for Charles when he signs his big contract,' it's almost a sense of relief to let go of all your negativity. Somewhere during our day, in some moment of reflection, when you're sitting in a room or just watching TV, you have to ask yourself, 'Why do I do this? Why do I lie to my friends and what makes me do it?' I used to be the biggest liar in the world. And I thought, why? Because I'm ashamed of where I come from and I'm ashamed to speak the truth. Now I only tell the truth."

Why should he be ashamed? I don't have to feel bad about having a nice house and a nice car. Hey, white people do it. That's what most people do. Sometimes, because of how we grew up, minorities have an inferiority complex, as if we're not supposed to have nice things. When I hear that Oscar de la Hoya isn't beloved by Mexicans, I think it's crazy. Why isn't he loved? Because he doesn't live in the barrio? Should we hate a black guy because he doesn't live in the ghetto? Or an Indian guy because he doesn't live on the reservation? That means he isn't real? Come on.

For some reason, minorities are so insecure that we don't support

each other. A guy does well in school, we call him a sellout. A guy moves to a nice neighborhood, they call him a sellout. When a white guy moves to a nice neighborhood, they call him successful. But being a successful minority means you carry a heavy burden. For George, being the only Latino in such a high-profile TV position, he has an obligation to carry the torch. Yes, it's pressure. But that's just how it is.

I always say that to Tiger Woods when he gets frustrated with the media and they criticize him for a bad stretch when he hasn't won any golf tournaments. Hey, that's just how it is. Yes, it's wrong. You just have to deal with it. You can't overreact. They don't say to Ernie Els or Phil Mickelson, "What's wrong with you?" when they don't win.

I think George had to get through all of this the hard way.

"I knew in high school that weed and drinking and stuff was going to be a problem genetically," he said. "I drank a lot in the nineties and was destroying myself. And I figured, you know what, I'm destroying myself by drinking, that's something I can control. Drugs, I was always afraid of. But alcohol I wasn't, and I enjoyed it. And at some point I thought, I'm only hurting myself and the people around me. Much like people do every day. Relationships would end. I started to lose friends. I started to realize that I was my biggest problem. I wasn't somebody that it was cool to be around. And I was going to do what my grandfather had done to the people who were around him: get drunk and isolate everybody and be mean. And I thought, 'You know what? I'm not going to go out like this.' I should learn from all the dudes in my neighborhood who had uncles and fathers who died early because of drinking. They drank themselves to death because they were unhappy with their lives—and what their lives had become. I thought, 'I'm not going to do that.'

"You don't have to dwell on history. You know people have given their lives and died in the fields, died running, died fearful deaths. People of color died so we could just vote. People died to live free, and if I don't pay some respect to the past, then what am I doing here? There's going to be some little Mexican kid who sees me when I'm old and he'll say to me, 'You know what? I'm a comedian. I just signed a deal to do a show and I saw you twenty years ago and you inspired me.' I still haven't forgotten Freddie Prinze. Right here, I've got his American Express card that his widow gave us."

We all have our heroes, our inspirations, and our mentors. The difference between George's business and mine was that he didn't get to hang with his mentors. When I first got to the Philadelphia 76ers, I had Dr. J and Moses Malone in the locker room, on the plane, at the hotel, telling me what to do. When you're a comedian, you're by yourself. Rodney Dangerfield wasn't traveling around with George Lopez. Eddie Murphy wasn't traveling around with him. Comedians are trying to make it on their own.

We all have what I call the screw-up gene in us. In order to keep it from taking over and ruining your life, you have to surround yourself with good people. It's easy to look around and say, "I can buy all the cars I want, I can load up on drugs." But you need people to keep you in check. If you don't get caught up in the excess, don't get sidetracked in the distractions, you can enjoy the good life.

"I joined this country club, Lakeside," George said. "I wrote them a check for $80,000. I get there to the bar. A member says to me, in a conversation over a margarita, 'Welcome to the club. Did you know that over ninety-five percent of our staff is Hispanic?' And I said, 'You know what that's going to make me? The king of the country club.' I tip everybody. I tip like Frank Sinatra. I tip everybody, 'cause you know what? It means more to them than just the $20, or $40, or $100. I'm going to go over and shake everybody's hand. 'How's everybody treating you?' I'll say to them in Spanish, 'Everybody treating you all right? Let me know if they don't.' And they start laughing. Then I insult them in Spanish. They laugh. And the guy sitting there having a martini is wondering, 'What are they doing, conspiring to take over?' "

If you're black or Latino, every time you go to a country club, you feel as if it's the last stronghold of racism. I don't feel uncomfortable . . . but I notice some tension. Some golf courses won't even hire blacks or Latinos. They don't want us on the premises at all. Not even as the help.

I've been at places where I've been the only black person there. You have to understand, baseball and basketball might have had unwritten rules against allowing blacks in their leagues, but golf had it in the books. It was known as the "Caucasian-only clause," and the Professional Golfers Association had it until 1961.

I know there are some places I'll never be accepted. There are some places I'll always be a nigger. There are people who hate themselves, and they hate blacks, Mexicans, and Jews even more. There are some places I'll never be accepted, some places where I can go to play but will never have a chance to join.

I've played at Shoal Creek, the country club in Alabama that nearly had the 1990 PGA Championship yanked away because it didn't have a black member at the time. But I know I can't join there. They have their guy already.

People say, "Do you feel like a token?" I say, no. Can you imagine if Jackie Robinson, or Earl Lloyd in the NBA, had said, "I don't want to be a token?" Because if there isn't somebody to be a token, there'll never be a second or a third.

I take great pride when I play these courses. Because I know it annoys the hell out of people. They might be calling me a nigger behind my back, but I just think, "You might not want me around, but I'm here now."

And we're not going anywhere.

You think you'll ever hear George Lopez make apologies for who he is? I love the fact that he's doing it his way. George wanted to make sure that if he was going to have a show about his people, it would be influenced by his people. He just had the power to do something about it.

Now, you've got to be fair. I would never hire a black man just because he's a brother. He's got to be qualified. But I think minorities are more fair than whites when it comes to hiring. I was on a panel at the National Association of Black Journalists' convention one year, and I noticed that all of the cameramen working at the event were white. I joked about it: "All the journalists are black, but the cameramen are white?" But I think black people are more fair than white people when it comes to race.

George is at that stage where he only wants to present the truth and doesn't care about the consequences. You've got to do what's best for you. You've got to say what you want to say. For instance, I'm pro-choice when it comes to abortion. I've said that on television, and each time I've received thousands of phone calls and letters. What am I supposed to do? The guy asked me a question. I can't worry about who I'm going to offend or upset.

I don't think I'm right all the time. But if you don't have an opinion, that makes people mad. Because then what you're telling them is "I'm more worried about my endorsements and my money than I am about doing something."

People have called on Tiger Woods and Michael Jordan to share more of their opinions instead of giving the safe answers. Believe me, they could be bolder if they wanted to. Both of those guys have a half billion dollars. They could afford whatever financial hit their image might take. And they don't realize that negative publicity is going to come regardless. They might as well be their own man, their own person.

Like George Lopez, I feel really good about being my own man. I love it when people tell me: "I don't agree with you all the time, but I respect the fact that you say it."

That's all I want from anyone.

GO DOWN, MOSES

RABBI STEVEN LEDER

Steven Leder is senior rabbi at the Wilshire Boulevard Temple, where he presides over one of the most influential synagogues in Southern California, one whose congregation includes major film producers and network executives. Rabbi Leder grew up in Minnesota and went to college at Northwestern, which makes him midwestern through and through. (Coincidentally, it was while talking for a couple of hours at his office in Los Angeles one afternoon that he and Mike Wilbon figured out that not only were they at Northwestern at the same time, but they hung around with a few of the same people, and more than likely had dinner with each other twenty-five years ago.) So, it's a long, long way from where I grew up in Alabama. But sometimes people can grow up a lot farther away than we did and be connected in the way we think.

When I was a kid, my mother and grandmother made me pay close attention to the civil rights movement, made me watch all of the footage. I always noticed that whenever black people were getting blasted with fire hoses, whenever the dogs were attacking them, there were white people right there with them, taking all the hits. There have always been great white people helping out. There always will be.

I didn't grow up around Jewish people, had met very few until my first agent, Lance Luchnick, was in my house and said, "I'm Jewish." I said, "What does that mean?" I didn't even know it was a religion.

Because I didn't know about it, I didn't have any preconceptions or bias. I judge every individual on his own merits. Lance wound up getting me in so many bad investments I was more than a million dollars in the hole. I don't hold that against Jewish people. That's about Lance. There's also probably a million dollars out there that I've loaned to black people and they haven't paid me back. That doesn't mean it's a black trait. It's not right to think that way.

I liked Steve Leder right away for a lot of reasons, but one in particular struck a chord with me. One of his great interests over a number of years has been the lack of dialogue on race in America. "To bring people together is a conscious, positive act," he said. "Doing nothing is easier and certainly keeps people apart. It's easier to do nothing than to do something. Inertia is easier." He doesn't just talk to hear himself. He wrote a critically acclaimed book, *More Money Than God: Living a Rich Life Without Losing Your Soul*. Of course, he counsels. Wilshire Temple operates an elementary school. He's a believer, like I am, in dialogue. It seems he believes that the bigger the problem, the more important the dialogue, which is where our discussion began. At least in the 1970s and 1980s, race was something people talked about. Archie Bunker might be a fictional character, but there was nothing fictional about the conversation. But that's faded for the most part. You can't talk about race in polite company because the very topic makes too many people nervous. But I believe that if the conversation doesn't put you a little on edge, you're probably not talking about anything of great substance.

Rabbi Leder sounded emotionally invested in the dialogue on race when he said: "I've spent a good deal of my time and energy working on it. I've had a lot of frustration working on it, too. It takes awhile to get to the point where groups can even have dialogue because individual communities have so many concerns.

"I remember a conversation I had about fifteen years ago, when I was in only about my third year here, with Reverend Chip Murray. I was frustrated, which I expressed to him. I'm, like, twenty-six years old. I'm eager to get at this issue. I told him, 'Hey, I'm ready to bring all these Jews to the table, ready to talk about blacks and Jews. . . . Chip, what's the deal? Why aren't you guys at the table with me?' And he said to me, 'Rabbi, do you know what most blacks think about Jews?' And I said, 'No, I don't.' And he said, 'They don't.' And I knew right away what he was saying to me. He was saying that getting along with Jews is so far down the list of priorities because we have so many gigantic problems. He was saying, 'Don't take it personally. It's just that you—this particular thing at that particular moment—are simply not that big of an agenda item.' And he was being frank with me. He wasn't being dismissive or rude. He was just saying, 'We have so many other problems to worry about.' But I've never stopped being interested in that dialogue. I've never stopped. At twenty-six years old I would go to these black–Jewish dialogues. I was the youngest person in the room then. I've been at it eighteen years, and I'm still the youngest person. What does that tell us?

"Like most things," he said, "it's about finding the right partner. Our temple has two campuses; this is the fairly new campus. We also have a seventy-five-year-old campus five minutes from South Central Los Angeles. The gas station across the street from the temple was burned to the ground during the riots, the Rodney King riots or civil disobedience or whatever you want to call it. The gas station across the street was burned to the ground. The neighborhood was in flames. That's where that other campus is, and it's been there for seventy-five years. When I first came to the temple I was handed a portfolio that included our interfaith work, which is about getting along with all the churches up and down the street, the preachers and ministers. And as part of that, I got to know this guy named Ken Flowers, who is now in Detroit. Kenny and I became really close friends; he was the pastor at Messiah Baptist Church in South Central. We're the same age, we had little kids the same ages. Our wives bitched about us the same way because it's not easy being married to a clergyperson. And through Kenny I met Tavis Smiley.

"Tavis, then, was working for Mayor Tom Bradley. I'm a couple of years older than Tavis, who grew up in Bunker Hill, Indiana, about forty-five minutes away from where my wife grew up in Marion. So Tavis and I hit it off. He and Kenny, at the time, were running something called L.A.'s Young Black Professionals. And at the same time I was running something at the temple called Young Professionals. My group consisted of a couple hundred yuppies—doctors, lawyers, bankers—people in their twenties and thirties without kids. Tavis and Kenny had the same thing going with black professionals. I don't remember who said it, but it was obvious that we needed to do some things together. So we created a program called Crossing the Line. I got the temple's resources to bankroll this thing and we started planning activities together. We had a pulpit exchange. I spoke at Kenny's church and our people went there. And he came to the temple and members of his congregation came to temple. And then we planned a conference, a weekend at UCLA called Crossing the Line, where we had workshops and picked things that we felt would unite us in our conversations rather than divide us. We didn't start with the hard things, which I think is an important thing when you're building a dialogue. It's like a marriage, you know? When you first date you don't start talking about your faults. You start with the easy stuff.

"We each talked about being a distinct minority in America, something members of both groups know plenty about, right? We had a workshop on responsibility to one's own community versus our responsibility to the larger community, which is an issue we all struggle with. We had one on intermarriage, something we all deal with. There's a lot of prejudice in the Jewish community about marrying a non-Jew. Just like there's prejudice in the African community about marrying a white person, an Asian person, a person of a different race. So we picked these things where we both have some common ground to talk about and prevent it from becoming overly radicalized. And we did everything fifty/fifty. The night before, we had a party and we had a black comedian and a Jewish comedian entertain. The food was half African American soul food and half deli. I mean we did everything the right way. Everything was planned together and we got two hundred young blacks and Jews talking.

"Very recently, Tavis and I were having dinner at my house and we were talking about this, reminiscing about one of the most significant things we've ever done in our lives. I still bump into people in airports and in airplanes, and through e-mails, who were involved with this program back then. All of us, everybody I've ever gotten feedback from, look so fondly on it. And then this program—Crossing the Line—wins an award. Kenny and I went to Washington, D.C., to receive it, and it got so much more attention. The next thing we did was start planning a trip to Africa and Israel. *Roots,* right? Go to Ghana, go to Jerusalem. I'm going to see where your roots are—not that everyone's roots are in Ghana, but it was safe at the time to go there. So we picked Ghana, stable, safe environment. And we're going to go to Israel. And we had it all worked out. The only thing was we were all in our twenties and nobody had any money, so it couldn't work. Other than that it was a great idea. Now we could probably pull it off—and maybe we will. But L.A.'s Young Black Professionals sort of went away as Ken went to Detroit and Tavis went on to other things, including running for city council, which I helped him do.

"In his campaign, I got the Jews behind him. I told people, 'This is a guy who will never stab us in the back. He will never turn his back on the Jewish community; he's our friend.' And we supported Tavis. But he lost. He was trying to do something pretty big. I always told Tavis, 'If you want to go into politics, go to law school and do it right.' But Tavis figured out, of course, there's no money in politics and he went into media. And he decided to make some money and that's cool. But after the group fell apart, I said, 'What am I going to do to keep this work going?'

"Well, there's an organization here in L.A.—and I know it exists in other big cities—called One Hundred Black Men, which is older guys, psychiatrists, lawyers. A guy named Jim Black was the president of it. And I had a group here called One Hundred Jewish Men. So we started bringing those two groups together in the late 1990s. We started doing things with them. I had our guys creating internships during the summer for the kids they were mentoring through high school. But Jim's replacement as president wasn't interested in doing things with the Jews, and that fell apart. Since then, I've had a very difficult time finding the right market. But we keep pitching. Right now, we're trying to help coordinate a Jewish-Christian-Muslim trip to Israel."

Because I consider bigotry and racism the worst cancer of my lifetime, I wanted to have these kinds of conversations with people of influence. And I wanted this book to be balanced. I didn't just want a bunch of black people saying bad things about white people. I want to be positive.

Let's be real: Alabama can be a horrible place. It's my home, but it can be a horrible place. When you're beyond the year 2000 and blacks and whites don't live together, when you have a black homecoming queen and a white homecoming queen because people won't accept a homecoming queen of another race, that's a cancer. Rabbi Leder, as it turns out, has his own reasons for seeing bigotry as a cancer.

"I'm not sure what Freud would tell me if I was lying on his couch," he said. "But I can tell you this much. I grew up in Minneapolis, which was at the time very white. There was one minority kid in my high school, and she was Asian. But when I was about five years old I had polyps on my vocal chords and I needed surgery. I shared a hospital room with a little boy, black kid who was my age, five or six. I was only there for a couple of days, but he was the first black person

I had ever met. And we developed this little two-day friendship. His mom was great, his family was great. But I never heard from him again. Still, something, and I'm sure I know what it was, happened there. We have to start with the fact that I grew up in a racist family. I've written about this. My dad, who is one of the most wonderful guys in the world, doesn't know he's a racist, but he's a racist, right?

"I wrote this article for the *Jewish Journal* called 'The S Word.' Jews don't use the *N* word; they use the *S* word, *Schvartze*, which is a Yiddish/German word that means black, but it's derogatory. It is derogatory. It's the *N* word in Yiddish. So I wrote this article and talked about my father's linguistic racism. See, here's the crazy thing about my dad: He's the man who would offer a black man coming out of prison a job because it was the right thing to do. But he'd also call him a *Schvartze*. He hired a *Schvartze* for this and a *Schvartze* to do that. It's just another kind of racism. So I took the lid off that in the Jewish community, because the Jewish community is always talking about how we marched in Selma and we were heavily involved in starting the NAACP, and all that's true. We, Jews, brought Dr. King to Boston, which was the first time, I believe, that Dr. King came north. But it's also true that there's racism in the Jewish community. It's a more subtle kind of racism, but it's there. So I kind of took the lid off that in an article.

"Now why am I telling you this story? Because when I was in second grade, in Ms. Carlson's class, I told a joke that I had heard around the house. I didn't remember if it was my dad who said it or my uncle, but I told her this joke. I said, 'Ms. Carlson, why doesn't the United States annex Africa?' I didn't even know what annex meant. But I just kept going with it because I'd heard people laugh the day before. She said, 'I don't know,' and I said, 'Because then we wouldn't be able to say, Send them back to where they came from.' And she didn't laugh. I didn't understand why she didn't laugh because everybody around the house was laughing the day before. Now keep in mind I had no idea what the joke even meant.

"The next day—God bless her if she's still alive—Ms. Carlson started class by saying, 'Someone told a joke yesterday, and I know they didn't mean it this way, but it was terribly wrong.' And she gave us the racism lecture. I didn't know it was racism, I didn't know what it was. But it was, of course. And I felt so bad, just like a second grader feels bad, and I kind of made this internal promise in my head never to be fooled like that or to just accept blindly these things.

"Then I go off to college to Northwestern, where I felt very out of place. It was very WASPy. It was me, the Jew, trying to assimilate with Biff and Mary and Thomas III. I was there with all these WASPy white kids I had nothing in common with. I was lonely. I was home-sick. I felt totally out of place. The only kids I could befriend and feel close to were the black kids. I would go to eat my meals at Elder Hall. All the black kids sat in one corner. And I'd go over and sit with them because I didn't feel comfortable with anyone else, because I didn't feel . . . white. Looking back on it now, at the time, at age eighteen, 'white' didn't describe a color of skin. It had to do with the culture I grew up in.

"I was not white. I try to get this across in dialogue. I can't always get it across and not everyone believes me when I say it, but I believe every Jew understands it when I say it. When I say 'we're not white' in a group of Jews, every Jew in the world understands what I mean. I feel as uncomfortable walking down the street in Pasadena as blacks do. And Jews understand that. Now, I'm not about to suggest I'm subjected to anywhere near the level of bigotry that blacks are. No Jew in this country is. Anti-Semitism is virtually gone in America—not in the world, but in America. But I felt closer and more liked by these black kids at Northwestern than I did the white kids. I just felt connected in a way that I could not connect to the white people there.

"Obviously, I'm immersed in the Jewish world now and I feel very close to Jews, to my tribe, my people. I feel very deeply connected or I wouldn't do what I'm doing. But outside of that, the closest thing I know of to Jews in America are blacks. We have different problems, different issues. But there's something there that is very deep and real for me.

"In 1975 or 1976, when the UN passed a resolution equating Zionism with racism, there was a big rally at the University of Minnesota. I was fifteen, sixteen years old. They were saying, basically, that if you believed in Israel you're a racist. And what Israel represents to the Jewish people is not racism, it's survival. Pure and simple. So at this big rally, Hubert Humphrey was the speaker. And that guy could speak. He could have any job at any Baptist church in America. That guy was a great orator. He could *preach,* okay? Who else was it? Bayard Rustin comes out and starts singing 'Go down, Moses,' and it blew me away. Here's this black man up there singing a song that goes back to the Jewish roots of slavery, and I just felt this important connection.

"Now I think where we get into trouble is when we pretend it's more than it is. I've responded to Farrakhan on National Public Radio. Tavis did a two-part interview with Farrakhan, and he asked me to respond to Farrakhan. I presented that what he said was anti-Semitic—not the whole thing: 95 percent of what he said was pretty cool actually, but 5 percent was anti-Semitic. But something else I said in my response is that one of the things we both share is we have to move beyond being victims. That's a very threatening thing to say when you've spent a hundred years invested in being the victim. Charles, you and Mike didn't get to be where you are by being invested in being a victim. And I'm tired of Jews pretending to be victims when they aren't. It's the greatest time to be a Jew in America. Not in France, not in Israel. But in America, it's the greatest time to be a Jew, ever. And I think that's a more mature constructive level at which to have this conversation than 'poor us.' There's almost no anti-Semitism in America, and every door is open to Jews in this country, period. Two Supreme Court justices, eleven senators, Jews make twice as much money as any other minority in America. Who are we kidding? We're not victims. Why are we pretending we're victims?

"I kind of said that to Farrakhan. I said, 'You, too, have to stop pretending you're a victim, 'cause you're not a victim.' And this is I think the next frontier of African American–Jewish dialogue: How do we move beyond that original bond of victimization? Yes, we were both victimized. But how do we really move beyond that to a more realistic reflection of where we are today, a healthier reflection of where we are today, and a more mature reflection of where we are today? How do we do that? That's what I'm interested in now. And my problem is that I don't know who to talk to.

"Maybe there are a lot of things the churches could do to address that. We run summer camps. We have an elementary school. We have a nursery school here. So we're full of kids. But if you don't build the product that people want for their children, they're not coming to church. They've got to think about getting people to church Monday through Friday, not just Sunday.

"I'll tell you the other thing I've sort of struggled with: Does it matter if the grassroots are talking? Does that matter? Does it matter that everyday ordinary African Americans and everyday ordinary Jews are talking with each other? You know what? I think it does matter. But at the very least we've got to be sure that the leaders are talking to each other. And I don't even think that's happening."

Part of the problem is that it's getting more and more difficult to identify the leaders. And we need leaders. Most people are followers. I'd run through a wall for Muhammad Ali, Malcolm X, Martin Luther King, or Medgar Evers. As much as I love our prominent black leaders today—such as Colin Powell, Jesse Jackson, Barack Obama—none of them inspire those same type of feelings. And as Rabbi Leder mentioned, Louis Farrakhan, a popular figure in the black community, has upset Jews with some of his comments. So he would not be the one they would seek out for conciliation.

I think there's no clear-cut leader in the Jewish community as well. There are divisions within the Orthodox, Conservative, and Reform ranks of the religion. Even Joseph Lieberman, who ran for vice president under Al Gore in 2000 and was an early-round presidential candidate in 2004, could not lock up the Jewish vote.

We need someone to get the message to the rank and file on both sides that we have such a common history. Rabbi Leder really enlightened me about the depth of the connections.

"One thing we share is the prophetic tradition," he said. "The Bible, both the Hebrew Bible and the Christian Bible, contains the writings of the prophets. Amos who said, 'Let justice roll down these waters and righteousness as a mighty stream. . . .' That's a tradition we share. 'Moses, let my people go' is a tradition we share. God punishes racism in the Torah. Moses is married to a black women, a

Kushite—Kush means Ethiopian in Hebrew—and when his sister Miriam and his brother Aaron criticized him for that, they're struck down with leprosy. God punishes racism in the Bible. God does not look kindly upon racism. And a lot of Jews don't know that. It's not an accident Jews were there. We share this tradition. A lot of blacks and a lot of Jews don't know that. We should know a lot more, and we would if there was more dialogue.

"You want to know when that broke down? What I believe is it broke down for a good reason. It broke down I think because blacks wanted to run their own show. They didn't want a bunch of Jews running the NAACP anymore. They were right. I think that's a huge part of it. The next thing I think happened is that the Jewish community turned inward for its own reasons. One, Israel was born and was threatened in 1967 and was threatened in 1973—Israel almost lost that war in 1973. Plus, we had the problem of Soviet Jewry, millions of Jews in the Soviet Union being oppressed, imprisoned, and killed. So the Jewish community turned inward. We decided, 'We have got some of our own problems, serious problems that we've got to solve. This is a luxury talking to you other people.' That's a part of it. And I also think that a part of it is that we were in diapers in the sixties, and us talking to our kids about the civil rights movement is like talking to them about the Peloponnesian war. It's ancient history. My children are a long way from the Civil War, my children are a long way from Selma. Do you know how old you thought your parents were when they were in their forties? How old did you think your parents were when they were our age? Ancient, man, I mean near death. Well, that's what our kids think we are.

"I'll tell you one other thing I think is very difficult. I think people naturally respond to oppression and want to help. It's getting impossible for Jews to claim oppression in America and it's getting harder for African Americans to claim oppression in America in my kids' eyes. In my son's eyes, African Americans are rich and powerful, and that's because the images being projected are that of having been accepted, of being influential, of being rich and being powerful. And to some degree that's all true. Although it's like Chris Rock says, 'Shaq is rich. The man who writes his check is wealthy. Here, son, here's $20 million.' So there's a difference between wealthy and rich.

"My kids go to school with Denzel's kids and Magic's kids, you know. They know not all blacks have that kind of wealth. But the blacks they know are that wealthy. They know there's poverty, they know there are gangbangers. But those aren't the blacks they see. And who are the blacks that whites, in the main, see? Who comes into their lives? I worry about what kids are exposed to. I worry that the images they see don't reflect the reality of America . . . the reality in the world. I took my kids a few months ago to Cambodia. It's the second poorest nation on earth. People eat bugs there, insects. I mean it is poor. And there isn't that kind of poverty in America, thankfully. Go to Haiti, go to Cambodia, go to the Sudan—to the Darfur. We do have to work together. That's why it's broken. I think the world is broken, in large part because everybody is in their own little bubble. We're balkanized.

"But I'll tell you something else that has eliminated the basic discussion about our differences. If I was ever president of the United States I would spend all my time trying to figure out what to do about the virtual disappearance of the leveling and socializing institutions in America, the things that brought us together. There were two that were more important than all the others: the public school system and the military. Those were the places where everybody had to get along.

You had no choice. It's where people who first thought they were so completely different rubbed shoulders with one another. That's where it happened. It happened in the army and it happened in the public schools, because for so long in the United States, everybody went to the army and everybody went to public schools.

"Now you have this apartheid situation in America. It's not racial as much as it is economic. There is economic apartheid in America. The rich kids go to school one way, except for the few poor kids who sneak in on a scholarship—maybe 10 percent—and the poor kids go to school another way. The rich kids don't go and fight and die; the poor kids go and fight and die. The poor white kids and the poor Hispanic kids and the poor black kids. So that's another part of the problem, another thing we have lost, the socializing. The socializing institutions created a fabric. I'm not saying there wasn't bigotry and sexism and racism, because of course there was. But still, we fought together and we went to school together—that's no longer true. You used to go to school with the kids in your neighborhood and that isn't true anymore either, not for rich kids anyway. They go where they get in. They go to these fancy private schools and it's the implosion of the public schools that has balkanized America beyond what may be reparable."

Private schools are among the worst things that ever happened to America. It separated our kids. Do you really think rich people would stand by and let the schools deteriorate if their own kids had to go there? I agree with the rabbi: It has become apartheid. There's no other way to describe it.

And serving in the military is an honorable way of life. But it's a hard life. You might get housing and other benefits paid for, but you

might be making only a couple of thousand dollars a month. You can't support too many family members with that salary. You can't buy a house in the big cities with that salary. I know there are programs, such as the Reserve Officers Training Corps, ROTC, that will help our troops-to-be get through college. But what about their kids? I think the deal should be if you serve our country, we'll put a kid through college. Serve eight years, we'll put two kids through college.

Right now the armed forces are too financially unappealing. If you're well off, you have to *really* love your country to enlist. And when there's an economic gap, you're also likely to find a racial gap. So the military doesn't reflect our society. About 25 percent of the army is black. That's more than double the percentage of the black population in the country. And the higher the percentage of black people in the army, the less the opportunities for other races to be exposed to each other, to share meals and barracks and drill lines together.

Rabbi Leder talked about this lack of interaction. Without that dialogue, black people and Jewish people don't understand exactly how each other's community operates.

"Here's one of the things that is important to understand about Jews if you're African American," he said. "In the Jewish community, publicly criticizing our leaders is totally acceptable. It's sport. It's a pleasant pastime in the Jewish community to be publicly critical of Jewish leaders. That's like totally okay because that's the way the body politic in the Jewish community works. So when an African American leader says something inappropriate or anti-Semitic or racist, Jews expect that the African American community works the way our community works. If a Jew gets up and makes a statement like that, the Jewish community is all over him. He's a moron. He's an idiot. He doesn't represent us. So when Farrakhan says something terribly anti-Semitic, or when Jesse Jackson one time in his life—I think he's an amazing man—sticks his foot in his mouth, the Jewish community expected the African American community to handle that the way we would have handled that. But that's not the way the African American community works. You don't take your leaders to task publicly, the way we do. Things are done differently, the way African Americans want them handled. It makes it difficult when I'm trying to facilitate dialogue, but I wind up telling Jews, 'It gets handled, trust me. But it gets handled the way it needs to be handled in their community just like we handle it the way we want to in ours.' "

I worry about that, however, because sometimes we—black people—ought to hold ourselves more publicly accountable. There's a difference between criticism and ridicule. And you don't have to try to embarrass somebody because you disagree. But when people of whatever race are insensitive to black folks, we want others of their race to condemn them . . . or at least condemn what they said that we find offensive. We need to be able to do that as well. So many black people got angry with Bill Cosby for coming out and making the observations he did about some of the stuff that's wrong in our communities. One of the things I was sorry to see go was Chris Rock's weekly show. Not only was it the funniest show on TV and really entertaining, it gave Rock a political forum and he didn't just slam white folks, he slammed us. And I thought it was great. It was necessary. He would have one of his rants and didn't care if the guy—it could be Reverend Jackson—was sitting right there next to him.

It's possible, though, that the conversation about race is going to become so difficult we won't be able to define it so easily in terms of

black and white. Rabbi Leder says he is convinced that "America is becoming so multicultural that there will be no 'them' or 'us' anymore."

"There's just us, all of us," he says. "I'm a rabbi, not a social historian. But I think if society were to bare its ugly teeth, its vicious ugly side, what it would be is class warfare, not racial or anti-Semitic. I think it will be rich against poor. That's what I'm most worried about. I think that is the real danger in America. We're becoming more and more like an apartheid society based on economics."

I'll take it even a step further. I believe poor folks, black and white, have been virtually brainwashed to hate each other. Not only are they going to be successful if they band together, but America is dominated by financial subcultures now. Poor folks go their whole lives fighting each other, while small groups of people, laughing all the way to the bank, carve up the whole big pie of money. Man, you talk about divide and conquer. You've got too many people not working together, believing race is their problem when poverty and bad schools are their problem, and before you know it, there's a small group of people who have all the money. As long as they keep the poor people divided, those poor people are never going to be able to get a decent-size piece of the pie.

"My point," Rabbi Leder said, "is that we need to redefine the conversation at a content level that is a better reflection of today's reality. I'll give you an example. My daughter went to a school called Center for Early Education. It's got black kids, white kids, Asian kids. But they're all basically rich. She was showing me her class picture a few years ago and she said, 'Look at the funny smile on Lena's face.'

So I said, 'Well, which one is Lena?' And she said, 'The one with the pigtails.' And I said, 'Which one? There's like four girls with pigtails there.' And she said, 'The one in the third row.' And finally she said, 'The black girl.' Like that was the last way that she would have thought of Lena, not the first way. Our generation, we would have said, 'Well, she's the black girl.'

"The trick now is understanding there's a balancing act. There are things very much the same about us that we need to recognize and affirm in each other and appreciate. But we also need to infer differences. And that's also okay and can be positive. I think for Tavis and me to have this friendship and never talk about the fact that he's black and I'm white would be dishonest to the friendship, because that's part of not just the friendship but the world we live in. We are different in some ways. We're not identical, so I think it's also got to be okay to talk about race. I don't think we're color-blind.

"But sometimes the sense of self isn't racism but atavism. Sometimes it's about us. Sometimes—and I'll put this in the context of being a Jew—the most important thing to us is our fellow Jews. Judaism is what matters. 'Survival of the Jewish people is what matters.' 'We're what counts.' It's 'Us, us, us.' That can create a problem. It happens with all of us. People decide that the only thing that matters is their own group. It's a kind of ghettoization. And it can be a problem. Even if it's not racism, it creates these barriers, a distance, a divide.

"But it's nonetheless part of the issue we need to be discussing. I think any new dialogue will have to look at race and beyond the question of race to see the problem in a more holistic, organic fashion. It's what are we going to do about the loss of these leveling socializing institutions in America? What are we going to do about the economic apartheid in America? Racism is a part of what creates this barrier, but it's only a part of what create this barrier. It's the economics that creates the barrier. It's in some cases language and linguistics that create the barrier. Look at what's going on in Montreal, right? In this country now it's also religion. I can't tell you how many people have framed what's happening since September 11 as a clash of civilization: the world of Islam versus the world of Christianity or Judeo-Christian versus Islam. So I think it transcends race, you know. You can't really isolate race without dealing with religion. You can't really isolate race without dealing with economic factors.

"I've been all over the country talking to people about money. People will talk about sex. They'll talk about hemorrhoids. But ask a group of men to share their net worth with each other? That isn't happening! First thing I do when I talk to groups about money is I walk in and say, 'I'd like everyone to just take a minute and turn to the person next to you and share your net worth.' Everybody laughs. They laugh because all of us, no matter how decent or good we are, because of the culture in which we live, succumb to believing that, in some small way at least, our net worth and our self-worth are related. That's destroying our sense of what it means to be a human being. If I were to say to you, 'Mike, what's he [Charles] worth?' . . . all our minds have gone to the same place. We all believe I'm really asking how much money do you have. And yet we also all know, because we're three good guys, that really we know better. We know that what a person's true worth is has nothing to do with how much or how little money he or she has. But we can't help ourselves because that's our culture. And that's twisted.

"The economic piece of our interactions is very important," Rabbi Leder said, "but I see it as the last taboo subject in America. I'm trying to stimulate that conversation with varied degrees of success. Tom Waits has a song on *Mule Variations* and the refrain is: You 'got to get behind the mule in the morning and plow.' And I identify with that, too. Every day, the thing I can do is get behind the mule and plow.

"One of the things we're discovering about bigotry today is it's more difficult to fight because it's harder to identify. It's more complex and more subtle, and therefore more difficult to root out than 'You can't eat here,' 'You can't vote,' 'You can't own property.' That's easy to identify. 'You can't live in this neighborhoood' is easy to get at and eliminate. But what's different is it's more deeply embedded. Instead of a tumor you can cut out—if you want to use the cancer analogy—it metastasizes. It's sprinkled here and there throughout the body politic of America, and therefore it's much more difficult to treat. And it's much less glamorous to treat. You don't get on the news for improving black–Jewish dialogue.

"Racism and bigotry today is a much harder enemy to fight. It's not unlike the problem Israelis have now. Israel is very good at fighting conventional wars. They know how to do that. For fifty years they've built machinery and operational structure to do that. But when you have people who are willing to strap bombs on themselves and walk into cafes and blow themselves up, what can you do? You know that tenth plague in Egypt, before pharaoh let the Jews go, was the plague of darkness. And the rabbis asked, well what was so terrible about the plague of darkness? And the answer they gave is that people didn't recognize one another's faces. In other words, they couldn't see the humanity . . . and once you get to that point, it's over. When you can't recognize the humanity in another person.

"But here's the good news about America to me, even with all its problems. I do think that tolerance is a value that is upheld by most

Americans. I believe that if you scratch deep enough beneath the surface, you'll find some bigotry in me. You will. I'm a product of my own environment. And if I scratch deep enough, I'd find some bigotry in you, some prejudice, maybe sexism, perhaps anti-Semitism. But if we scratch even deeper in most of us, I hope, I believe that we'd find someone who also knows that it's wrong. I have it, but I know it's wrong. And that's why I'm hopeful. I'm not pessimistic about human nature. I believe human nature is essentially good. I really do. There are a lot of barriers that get in the way of us manifesting that goodness, but I couldn't do what I do if I didn't believe human beings were essentially good. I couldn't get up in the morning."

I could sense Rabbi Leder's drive to do good that got him out of bed in the morning. And I could see how he can sleep comfortably at night, knowing he's doing the right thing. It's impossible to spend time with him without gaining knowledge. He's that brilliant.

Before we started talking I didn't know Jewish people had such a key role in founding the NAACP. And I'm in my forties. I bet most people under thirty have no idea.

If black people and Jewish people do consider their links, they tend to think about their oppression—the Holocaust, slavery. Comparisons are beside the point: It's deep, deep pain, any way you look at it.

But you can't go forward unless you get out of the past. The rabbi was very candid that for most Jews, hey, things are all right. Jewish people have moved on, no question.

Black people need to realize that we have it so much better as well. Most young black people have not experienced racism directly in their face. Maybe they've been called "nigger" a few times, but they haven't experienced real racism. The stuff our ancestors went through—not just slavery, but Jim Crow and the battles of the fifties and sixties—now that's racism. For an eighteen-year-old to be walking around now, talking about how he's being mistreated, that's just bull.

Now it's the subtle fight, the glass ceiling, or the closed door. But if black people have made it, they have to go back to the neighborhood and help out. And if Jewish people have made it, they can't forget those who still are struggling.

It's like the suggestion I once made to the NBA. They were running those "Stay in School" ads, but when I asked them to show me what programs were in place, they didn't have anything for me.

I've always thought they could hire high school kids to work for them in the summers, then pay their way through college. By the time they graduated they'd have four years to learn the business, could learn it inside and out, then come work for you. That's like a no-brainer.

I was struck by Rabbi Leder's desire to help. He feels a need to make a difference. It reminded me of a commercial they used to run, with two kids walking on a beach where hundreds of starfish had washed ashore. One of the kids picks one up and throws it back in the water, and the other kid teases him, saying: "You can't help all of those." And the first kid says, "You're right. But I can help that one."

THE NEXT LEVEL
ICE CUBE

Ice Cube has gone from writing rap lyrics in ninth grade to writing screenplays for major movies. He's gone from playing parties organized by another Southern California teenager, Dr. Dre, to performing with probably the most political, controversial, and uncompromising group of rap's early history, N.W.A. He has made the smoothest transition imaginable from being an enemy of the FBI (not a rap group, but the Federal Bureau of Investigation) to a star of mainstream movies like *Three Kings* and the 2002 hit *Barbershop*. Cube, still in his mid-thirties, has already appeared in more than thirty movies, been executive producer of a couple, and received a half-dozen credits for his screenwriting. He isn't afraid of work—he once went to Arizona to study architectural drafting. But even after he left N.W.A., it was clear his heart was still in the art of expression, and on his own he continued to take lyrical stances as a revolutionary rapper.

Depending on who you talk to, his lyrics were either ground-breaking or homophobic and misogynistic. He was at times called a racist because of his lyrics, yet built a large following among white rock devotees. The range of his work makes it difficult to even know where to start when talking to or about Cube. But the idea wasn't to make him explain his lyrics, but to get him, as perhaps the most in-fluential and compelling rapper-turned-actor, to talk about how in the world rap has gone from an underground, off-the-radar, in-the-neighborhood form of expression to an art form celebrated around the world, and how it has created some of the biggest stars in both music and entertainment.

Whatever people might say about rappers, these guys never got the credit or respect they deserve for bringing the races together. They should be rewarded for that. Sports and music bring blacks and whites together more than anything else I know. Especially hip-hop music. It doesn't even need its own category anymore. Hip-hop music is mainstream; mainstream is hip-hop.

People talked about rap music in quotation marks when Run-DMC helped popularize it by hooking up with rockers Aerosmith on "Walk This Way" in 1986. But most white folks still weren't listening to rappers. They didn't get all the credit they deserved.

When N.W.A.—with Ice Cube, Dr. Dre, Eazy-E, Yella, and Ren— came out with their breakthrough album *Straight Outta Compton,* that's when white kids started coming to rap. And it wasn't a com-promise. It was a raw look at life in the 'hood, and for some reason it took off. They'll never get the full credit for that. But they know what

they did. And that ability to get people of different races to buy the same thing is one of the main things I wanted to talk about.

"I've been in the game for a while, you know? I've been acting since 1990, which is crazy to me. And we've been doing music much longer than that," Cube said as he sat in his trailer, preparing to shoot scenes that afternoon for *Are We There Yet?*, a movie released in 2005. For a teenager, someone who is now fifteen or seventeen years old, Ice Cube is an actor, not a rapper. "People started to really hear of us in 1988, '89, but we started in '85," he said. "It's coming around on twenty years in the business for me, and I'm thirty-five, so it's been awhile.

"In terms of understanding how this all happened, where the popularity came from, the kids of course jumped on what was a relatively new form of expression before anybody else even knew what it was. Mainstream America started picking up on what we were doing, off the vibe of 'What the hell is this sweeping through our neighborhood?' I mean, it was to the point where it was something that you had to get, whether you understood it or not, whether you wanted to be part of the culture or not. People started telling me about all kinds of mainstream people trying to find *Straight Outta Compton*, listening to it, and basically trying to get a window into the neighborhoods that we were living in, trying to look over the fence at what we were doing. They didn't want to touch it. They condemned the hell out of it. But they were intrigued enough to start paying attention. So it was black people on it first, then people who were into hip-hop, black, Latino music, and then the white kids got ahold of it.

"Yes, it surprised me because if you know my personal story, you know we were attempting to do music for our neighborhood. That was it. Nothing else to it. We felt nobody outside our neighborhood would even care about what we were rapping about, you know? We just felt that this was happening in South Central Los Angeles. Nobody was ever going to talk about it 'cause nobody cared about West Coast hip-hop. But we were going to be stars in our neighborhood, for damn sure. That was our goal, to just be ghetto stars. And only people in our neighborhood had our tape.

"Then we went on tour, and this was our first time being exposed to the country. When else would I be in Mississippi or Tennessee or Chicago, you know? Our tour was behind Bobby Brown's. He'd be there, and two weeks later we would be in the same place. It seemed like we were just following him around. Y'all remember during that time Bobby was getting arrested for indecent exposure, getting taken off the stage? His show was wild during that 'My Prerogative' time. So we would run into these cops who would—and I'm talking about the chief of police in some towns—come bring ordinances backstage and tell us 'Yo, you can't do this, you can't do that, or you're going to be arrested.' In Cincinnati we got arrested. In Detroit we got run off the stage by the police department. Seriously, at a major concert they ran us off the stage. We'd be riding on the bus and hear other truckers say, 'What you got in there?' 'We got a rap group called N.W.A.' And you hear them saying stuff over the walkie-talkies like 'We got your watermelon truck over there.' I remember pulling into one truck stop in the middle of nowhere and getting back on the bus and a dude in the parking lot took a couple of shots at the bus."

Cube and all kind of rappers have stories like that from the early years of rap. But even though there was hard-core resistance to rap, the fact is that, in retrospect, the early rappers have to be given credit for reaching white kids who would never socialize with black

people otherwise. There were, and still are, so many social critics who stand up and talk about how bad rap is—and there are plenty of gangster lyrics that are criticized for good reason. But oddly enough, those artists and their songs brought people together who I don't think would have met otherwise. The total effect, when we look back on it years from now, might not be destructive, despite lyrics being negative and sometimes offensive. The total effect, if we're talking in the context of promoting discussion, might be something that's very positive.

I think Eminem's popularity as a white rapper in the black-dominated world of rap is another good sign. Black people are very accepting. If your music is good, black people will embrace it. The hip-hop world has been very hospitable. You won't see a black person dominate on the country charts the way Eminem has on the rap charts. We don't give a damn who's making the music; if it's good entertainment, we're going to enjoy it. I'm in my forties now, so my tastes lean toward the smoother R&B artists like Jill Scott and Brian McKnight. And I love the old Motown classics. But I'll listen to the new rappers who are actually singing about something, such as Kanye West.

While Ice Cube is more actor/screenwriter and producer now than anything else, the foundation he helped to build seventeen, eighteen years ago has produced an environment where rappers are recording with rock stars and country stars. Who on earth could see that coming? I think that's what people fear about anything revolutionary. You can't judge it accurately at the time. Some years have to pass before you can see its full effect. And what revolution ever comes about without some controversy, without criticism, without there being some things the people involved in the revolution would take back if they

had it to do over again? Considering how little dialogue there is between people of different races, rap has to be credited with going the other way and bringing some people together . . . even if that wasn't what the early rappers had in mind.

"When I started," said Cube, "what rap was really doing was allowing the youth to communicate with each other. Before rap, brothers out here [in Los Angeles] could care less what was going on in New York, Philly, D.C., Chicago. You'd hear about someone in the news, you could care less. But through these records, we know what's popping here, what's popping there. It's kind of our language. You had a generation, the one before mine, who are now in their forties and fifties, who are in positions of power and influence in their companies in the music industry. Now you have a brother in a movie like *XXX* [Triple X], you know what I'm saying? Just because rap has kind of churned the soil. The kid who might have been a total racist without rap now is like, 'Yo, I like this, I like this. I like everything that has to do with the rap culture. I like Spike. I like Jordan. I like Jay-Z. You know it's not so hard to accept.'

"In the eighties, when we went to Public Enemy concerts, especially in the late eighties, when they were at the height of their success, the crowd was very mixed, white and black. I remember when we went to Europe, it was crazy. White kids were into what we were doing. You started to feel like 'Okay, it's a new day. This generation can't be as bad as their fathers' after being exposed to us on this level and loving us as icons. Something has got to change, you know?' We're starting to see a little of the effects of that with black directors now directing all-white movies. Antoine Fuqua, for example, with *King Arthur.*

"I think three things transcend race: music, entertainment, and athletics," Ice Cube said. "After that you've got natural disasters and tragedies and accidents, things that happen where people don't think about race, where something is bigger than what somebody is and where somebody's from, where it's just teamwork because there's an emergency and we have to all get together. If everybody's house is burning down, then nobody cares what race you are. We're all going to go help, you know? Race truly goes out of consciousness, too, in sports. A dude makes a spectacular play and at that instant you don't care what color he is.

"It's pretty much the same in the entertainment industry. In a certain instance you could care less who it is because you just saw something and you loved it. Or in music. You hear a song you like and you just like it because it appeals to something in you and you don't give a damn who the artist is . . . not what race the person is, anyway. I think there are things that, on a day-to-day basis, transcend race and put us all on the same plane, you know? But to me it's also natural for people to root for their own kind to succeed, no matter who it is.

"I think we definitely root for our own kind. If you ever watch 'Family Feud' and there's a black family on, you know what I mean: You want them to win. You're watching 'Survivor' or one of these reality shows, and there's a natural tendency to want to see your own succeed. But the thing is, I think black people, people of color in general, can accept everybody succeeding. I think people of color can tolerate hearing about a white person who has had a downfall and then rises, but it just seems like from the white point of view, they could care less about what's going on with us, you know? It's really not on their radar. Whatever's in the news at that moment that's sensationalized, that's what they pick up on. But true feelings or interests or family issues . . . we're off the radar in the mainstream. They could care less. I think we definitely are the ones who have them on our minds more than they have us on theirs, you know?"

That's because we're living in their world, literally. That's how it is in the United States. Okay, it's evolving because the percentages of Hispanics and Asians are rising so quickly. But in the U.S., people of color are for the most part living in a white world, working for white people who, if they want to, can go their entire lives and not interact with black and Hispanic people. They never have the experience of having to go and ask a black person for a job, or having to modify their behavior to fit in with people of color. Some do. An increasing number of them do, in fact. But still, the majority don't have to interact, don't have to worry about behavior and how they might be perceived. And rappers, when they were observing their own world, never seemed to worry about any of that. They seemed free to let it rip.

"It's one reason I have a problem with black people who don't want to be themselves," Ice Cube said, "because they feel it makes black people in general look bad in front of white people. 'You're making us look bad!' You know, it might be true. They might be making us look bad. But the thing is white people really don't care how bad they look in front of us. They could care less. They don't think a white serial killer makes other white people look bad. They're never concerned with how they—the group—might look, you know? But we're always concerned, especially our elders, with what image we're putting out there. I think that's part of a bigger problem. I look at a black guy who knows he has a problem but spends all his time trying to mask it, cover it up. Don't want nobody to see it, don't want to admit he even has a problem, you know? So he never really starts dealing with the problem. So it's like all of our pain is starting to spill out into our culture, into our entertainment, through our athletes. Rich, successful, but still unhappy? Why? You know all these things? You can't mask them no more and there's no reason to. Let it all hang out, be yourself. Start dealing with some of these problems instead of sweeping them under the rug and always worrying about what white folks might think. To me, we're the first generation to deal with some of this stuff. Why lie and deny that we're in this condition, you know? Let it all hang out and start correcting our own problems by seeing that they're so bad."

Everyone has their problems, and I think that's what N.W.A. tapped into that made them so successful. There are a lot of white people out there struggling. Even the kids in the suburbs, driving the BMWs, they feel like they're missing something. It doesn't matter where you live, you're searching for *something*. Everybody in life is looking for something to help them get better. N.W.A. was rapping about drug dealers and gang members battling for turf or the police taking their power too far. But the themes were things all young people go through: They're struggling for recognition and respect among their peers, and they resist authority. N.W.A. didn't take anything from no one. Cube wrote most of the lyrics on the album, and as he once said, at that time, "I was mad at everything."

That anger, so raw and powerful, translated into triple-platinum album sales. What I liked about Ice Cube is that he didn't just stop there. The key is, when rappers make all their money, are they bettering the environment or are they just driving around drinking Cristal? You've got to take it to the next level.

You see what some of the other entrepreneurial rappers did with their money. They created clothing lines. Russell Simmons, whose Def Jam label was the home for Run-DMC and LL Cool J, among others, started Phat Farm. P. Diddy started Sean John. Jay-Z launched Rocawear. Black people, when they become successful, really have to make it grow even larger.

"What I've been lucky with in my career is I've always had some smart people around me who emphasize planning," Ice Cube said. "A lot of artists don't, at the beginning of the year, look forward and say, 'At the end of this year I want to be here. I want to do this. And what do I need to do during this year to make sure at the end of the year I'm where I want to be?' At the end of the year I want to be in a movie. Okay, so I start taking the steps to do that. I want to produce. I want to write. You know? So at the beginning of the year have a plan for what you want to achieve during this year. Doing so has kept me on the steady road of being able to seize opportunities. Each day I try to focus just on that day's task at hand, and not look at too much of the past, too much of the future. Everything I want in the future will be there if I take care of today and do today like today is supposed to be done. Then I figure one day I'll stop and look behind me and say, 'Hey, you know, there've been some good achievements along the way.' "

His greatest creative achievement, in terms of mass success, has been *Barbershop,* which, besides Ice Cube, starred Anthony Anderson, Sean Patrick Thomas, and Eve, another person whose roots are in hip-hop. It was that rare black movie: a comedy that was funny as hell but also uplifting. It didn't see the need to tear anybody down.

The characters weren't rich, but they had a certain dignity. And it didn't only appeal to black people. Black audiences alone didn't make _Barbershop_ a hit, which again goes to my point that viewers aren't as bigoted as the executives who make movies and television shows think.

"You know what I love about _Barbershop?_ It showed that black people don't all have the same opinions about the same things," Ice Cube said. "Put a topic on the table, get five different black men, they could be from the same generation, they could be from different generations, and everybody's gonna have a different opinion. I think it was important to show America that we don't all think alike. _Boyz 'N the Hood_ showed you a piece of gangsta life and the reasons why these young kids are growing up to be this, the circumstances that led to that life. Still, if you look closely at each of them, while they all grew up on the same block, they all had different outcomes. Doughboy could have been Tré with the right guidance. It showed that we weren't all just animals who come from nowhere, straight out of our momma's womb ready to kill, you know?"

But just like George Lopez found, if you're a minority performer trying to get work, you'd better be able to make people laugh.

"I hate that almost every comedian we have has to put on a dress at some point to be funny," Cube said. "That kind of irks me a little bit. A whole lot of people, black and white, would rather laugh than cry. Dramas are the hardest things to get made, especially dramas involving black people. I think it's because so much of what we've been through historically directly affects our plight now. I think it's hard for white folks to finance movies with those hard-hitting themes, sit through them, accept and swallow a movie like *Rosewood* that exposes the evils of their past. 'So let me get this straight: I'm going to finance a movie that's about to slap me in the mouth and make me feel bad when I leave? This serious stuff that might depress you or make you reflect on some times that sure ain't pleasant. It's too much shame and guilt, you know? And I'm going to fund this? I'm going to have to come to the premiere, I'm going to have to sit through it. I'm spending tens of millions of dollars to feel bad?' That's kind of ultimately where it starts to break up, you know? It's easier to get a comedy funded because you can laugh about your problems instead of cry about them.

"It's very limiting. It keeps us at a disadvantage, tells us there's a small range of things we can do. It limits opportunities. It's like these are your avenues, these are your resources. Dance, act, do a trick, run and jump—you know what I'm saying? Those are your choices, the only things you can hope for. That's it, that's the best you can offer America.

"Of course, the money has to be there to make the movie. Black movies hardly ever get the budget that white movies do. And it's based on what a movie is going to do internationally. You can have the top-grossing movie in the United States, but what is that movie going to do overseas? *Barbershop* was the top-grossing movie in the U.S. the weekend it came out, but when it went overseas it wasn't. So it's much more than a race thing; it's the dollar thing too."

The thing about the best rappers—and about people like Ice Cube who saw, early on, how the rap game was allowing for greater expression—is that they didn't just stop with rap. Whether we're talking about LL Cool J in his TV work or about Ice-T, who went from

recording "Cop Killer" to playing a police officer on NBC's "Law & Order: SVU," rap was not an end; it became a means to a new end. It's clear from Ice Cube's résumé that he works all the time, literally.

"I directed the movie *The Players Club,* which was released in 1998; I also wrote the screenplay. It took more than a year and a half. I've been grinding, man. I'm a grinder. I've gone from one project to the next. I think you have to work twice as hard and be twice as good, you know. And I think you have to be able to do twice as many things with less. But as far as getting talent—big-name talent—to direct . . . personal relationships with people can go a long way. That's really what this business is based on: a lot of personal relationships."

I respect the fact that Ice Cube took it to the next level. There comes a point where you can't rap anymore. Now he's a movie star. He's a producer. He can hire black actors and actresses, give people an economic opportunity. I have a great appreciation for that.

If you're selling records, that's power. If you're on television, that's power. Then it's just a matter of what you're going to do with it.

Bill O'Reilly and Rush Limbaugh—do they care about anyone else? They want people to watch their shows, they write a couple of books, but they're not going out in neighborhoods trying to help other people. That's just how it is. It's sad, but it's true.

If rappers aren't going to do anything but buy giant rims for their cars, they're just as guilty. Ice Cube has shown that by setting higher goals for yourself, you can be in a position to help others.

"I've noticed that a lot of people," he said, "when they start to look at you and your career and what you're doing, the fact that you're doing it is as impressive to them as what you've got to say about it. 'So, Cube wrote his own movie? Damn, he come out of the neighborhood like I do! Damn, he did?' Just the act of doing it now opens up a door for people who find that out. 'Damn, maybe I could do that or something like that.' Now you have more and more people writing or trying to get their own DVDs out or doing their own movies, and in the process, creating an industry. It's like rap created an industry for youngsters really to make it. Now, through film, it's starting to open up another avenue. Athletics was the first avenue where youngsters who didn't have much said 'Yo, I could be a part of that.' And before rap, don't even try to be an entertainer. You can't sing or dance. Don't even try. Now there's a chance to be true to whatever you are and say what you can when you can."

It's all about being open and receptive. Without white people taking to hip-hop, rappers would never have enjoyed these astronomical sales. Ignorant rednecks—or ignorant blacknecks—have not bothered to expand their minds. I love broadening my horizons. Ice Cube showed me just how far a vision can stretch.

THE BEST OF TIMES, THE WORST OF TIMES

MARITA GOLDEN

One of the coolest things about writing a book that relies on interviews is meeting people I might not have met otherwise, like writer Marita Golden. She's written novels, including a best-seller, *Long Distance Life,* and she's written and edited nonfiction books, one of which—*Saving Our Sons: Raising Black Children in a Turbulent World*—especially intrigued me for the purposes of our discussion. She's been a writer-in-residence at such universities as Brandeis, George Washington, Howard, and Hampton. She's been published everywhere, from the *New York Times* to Essence *magazine,* and she established and still heads the Zora Neale Hurston/Richard Wright Foundation, which presents the only national literary awards to college writers of African descent.

As a black woman and a mother, a lot of what Marita Golden thinks and writes about deals with the dynamics of race and black family life in America. We met in Washington, D.C., to talk about those things, starting with her perceptions of opportunity in America for black people at the beginning of the twenty-first century. It's my perception that it's the best possible time ever to be a person of color in America, yet we seem to be squandering many of those opportunities.

"It should be the best time to be black in our history," Marita agreed, "even though we have the highest unemployment rate in the black community that we've ever had, other than during the Depression. So many of our young men are warehoused. Prisons are the new housing projects. In many states, they will base the number of prisons they're going to build on the number of kids in inner-city schools who are in the third or fourth grade and are failing standardized tests. I think that, for our part, when we were fighting so desperately in the civil rights movement, we kind of made a trade-off. We wanted integration so badly that we traded off the things in our own community that were really valuable. We wanted to be integrated so desperately into the dominant society that we forsook the value systems that had gotten us through lynchings, through segregation. Now, we're lost. We have more opportunity now and less sense of who we are. And our primary institution historically, the church, doesn't respond in any meaningful way. So we're facing a spiritual crisis that I think is part of what makes us so vulnerable to the forces that have always been out to get us."

Marita Golden isn't the only person to suggest that we've lost our way in recent years. That's one of Bill Cosby's themes. I've been won-

dering if we're just in some kind of transition, but that's a notion she rejected.

"A transition," she said, "would suggest that there was movement, and it implies there's a direction. A transition to what? Bill Cosby challenged black people and they didn't want to hear it, but perhaps the most important thing about Cosby saying it is it starts a forest fire because 'Bill Cosby said it.' I've been really heartened by the second response to Cosby, when he went around the country to the inner-city communities where the young people and the mothers and fathers he was talking about actually live. He's gone to schools and auditoriums, and those mothers and those fathers have come to hear him speak and have said, 'Right on.'

"What Bill Cosby did is what too few people in our community do. He set a very high standard. Too often, in many parts of our community, we don't have standards anymore. Or the standards are all upside down. In some black communities, the person who witnesses a crime and calls the police—as a good citizen should—is considered a snitch. And the young man who doesn't have any children out of wedlock, he's asked what's wrong with him . . . 'Why you ain't got no babies?' My son gets asked this all the time.

"We've got problems with values and with our institutions. We're in another world on some issues. We're a community that acts like AIDS doesn't exist. A black community in which churches are *filled* with women, just *filled* with women, and yet women can't speak from the pulpit in the typical black church. These are churches in which women are voiceless, okay? Churches in which women have plenty of sons, but those churches don't do anything to save those sons. We're going to need more people like Cosby to shake up and hurt people's feelings in the name of saving our children and saying what needs to be said. I'm married to a high school teacher who works in the inner-city schools that are too often war zones, so I hear the stories of lowered expectations or no expectations for our children. Then, some very highly paid intellectual black person, whose child is in a private school, whose child is in an affluent community, gets on CNN and talks about Bill Cosby being misinformed. But that person is part of the problem. How can anyone say that Cosby, who dedicated his life to doing nothing but educating black people and children, hates black people or is misguided? We need *more* people willing to risk embarrassing us, for the sake of the larger issue."

I know exactly what she's talking about. It kills me that Cosby was left to do this and got so little support at the time. I saw articles quoting supposedly intelligent people who were ripping Cosby. I called Bill and said, "Hey, man, keep up the good work."

My question is, Where are the people who should have said these things ten years ago, fifteen years ago? When I was a kid, leaders weren't worried about being popular or people liking them. The preacher at your church said what he thought was the responsible thing to say, and if the congregation didn't like it, too damn bad. You didn't even think to trash your leaders. I'm always asking black people now: Where the hell are our leaders? Who are they? We had them in the 1960s and 1970s, even in the 1980s. But I don't see anybody really taking the tough stands now and rallying people. Chris Rock even does a routine where he talks about Martin Luther King in the fifties and sixties, Jesse Jackson in the seventies and eighties. Then Chris says that in the absence of obvious leaders, he has come up with the perfect candidate for the new leader of the black community. It's

a guy who has led black men for the last twenty-some years, he says, a guy who leads black men every night and gets them to move in one direction and have one common goal. Then Chris shouts out the name "Coach Pat Riley!" and black audiences go crazy. It's funny as hell, but it speaks to my point that there doesn't seem to be the kinds of leaders black folks grew accustomed to in the twentieth century.

"Well, I think that the concept of one prophetic leader of a people is outdated," Marita said. "I don't think that, in 2005, we can invest all of our hopes and dreams in one prophetic leader. We should be at a point now where we should have a community, a national community, full of leaders. We do have leaders, but I think many of them are confused. They're saying what they think young people want to hear instead of challenging them to be the best they can be and do the best they can do. We don't challenge them enough. So many of us have simply dropped the ball. We move into our half-million-dollar house, have the Jaguar, Benz, you know, why not? And who are the leaders our kids look up to? Their leaders are Ludacris, 50 Cent, and even in affluent communities young black males want to be thugs. Now what's that about? Is that proving that you're black? What is that about?"

There are so many mixed messages about what is black, about what is legitimate black behavior, about how you're supposed to act or talk. I hate that stuff. You don't have to take somebody's life to be a man and you don't have to be hardened to be black. Being black isn't defined by being a thug or having your hair braided or cornrowed or anything like that. When we were in Reverend Jackson's offices, he had all these

photos of Ali and Malcolm X and Martin Luther King. They were all immaculately dressed all the time. He said, "Look at these people. Now I will admit it, they did some crazy stuff behind closed doors. But we understood that when we were out in public, we represented something bigger." The notion that going to school is *acting white* **is insane. We're insulting ourselves. The notion that being a real father who participates in raising his kid is** *acting white* **. . . that's sick.**

"I'm not saying these issues, these patterns and syndromes, are exclusive to black folks," Marita said. "I do think it's important to not see these things as separate from the larger society. When I wrote *Saving Our Sons,* many white parents would come to me and say, 'I live in the suburbs. I'm scared for my child, too.' So there is a sense that all our children are at risk. The world has changed for all of us. But it's clear that in our community, there's an enormous amount of confusion among black parents about values and about identity. The people who have the courage have to start speaking out.

"I think we also underestimate how we are all still damaged by slavery. Everybody in this country—black, white, everybody—underestimates what it does to the psyche of a people to be enslaved for three hundred years, submitted to segregation for another however many years. We're still suffering the impact of that. We're still suffering the impact. I wouldn't want reparations; I want free psychological services for every black person in America, free education, no taxes, but free psychological services first. You cannot underestimate how we have passed down the psychosis of self-hatred and continue to pass it down, whether we're in Beverly Hills, or Mitchellville, Maryland, where I live, or the 'hood."

If there's no way we can have one prophetic leader, it makes sense that we're not going to have one agenda. I think what we're hearing is that all black people don't have the same interests. I don't know that other races are expected to go through life with just one agenda. In the 2004 election the analysts talked about how both Democrats and Republicans sought the Hispanic vote, so Hispanics don't seem to allow themselves to be simply defined as a voting bloc. And they seem to have various agendas. Is it legit to at least wonder if black people are too diverse now to speak with one voice and have one set of goals?

"That may be true," Marita said, "but I think the one common interest that we still have is fighting racism. You're not going to take that away. And I'm leery of comparing us to immigrants, no matter what color. We're the only people who didn't come to this country to better ourselves. We came here to better the lives of white people.

"I don't buy into the argument that we're so diverse that for some of us racism isn't an issue. I think that we may think racism isn't an issue, but it's a reality that affects us if we're applying for a mortgage, if we're trying to get a taxi, if we're trying to get into Harvard. It's there, whether we want to face it or not, and I think it's an illusion and a delusion to say that it's not. It's symptomatic of our psychological disarray that we buy into that. What the cohesiveness of the Jewish community teaches us, even as some people are Orthodox and some are Conservative and some might even say, 'Oh I'm not a real Jew,' but when it comes to protecting their interests, they're all Jewish people who understand the sense of community.

"First, I don't think we're in a state of integration when we know that the schools are just as segregated in America as they were in 1964. We know that housing is nearly as segregated as it was in 1964.

We're simply not an integrated society. Of course, I also think we have a tendency to romanticize how healthy we were in the days of segregation, real segregation. Then, black people worked together, we lived together, we were forced to do that and we couldn't integrate. But within those segregated communities, on Saturday night, black people would get drunk and pull out knives and razors. When I was growing up here in Washington and my parents owned boarding-houses, I remember that every Friday night—payday—the man would come home to the third floor and beat the crap out of his wife. This was 1954, and life was very much segregated, but we overestimate how healthy we were back then. I think we thought integration would give us dignity, but it doesn't. Yet what could we do? Were we to accept second-class treatment? Were we to accept legal segregation? We couldn't do anything *but* fight against it."

You could go forever on the argument of integration vs. segregation, and we won't. But what I feel happened is we presumed going to their schools, eating at their restaurants was going to level everything. And all it meant, really, was that we ended up going to school with them and eating at their restaurants.

"But then, you see, when we come back to our tribe, we often undercut it, destroy it, neutralize it," said Marita. "We don't necessarily sustain it. We've made some progress, but the issue is very, very, very complex. Even so, I would like to see more people asking more of our young people."

Ultimately, I think that's what we can agree on. That's not particularly complex: challenging youngsters the way people of my gen-

eration were challenged. I lived in a little rural town with one stop-light. And my mom said to me, "You're the first person from this fam-ily to go to college. Just don't embarrass me and don't mess it up." I remember that vividly. Danny Glover, whom I've talked to many times about this, often says, "You guys don't get it. I've lived my whole life, and I still don't want to embarrass my mom and dad." It's so simple yet so true. But Marita points out something else that's at work here, something that cannot be blamed on any other community of people.

"For thirteen years," she said, "I was a single parent. Our commu-nity is filled with overworked mammas and long-gone daddies, and one of the things I think needs to be talked about is the support sys-tem that these mothers need to raise these sons. There's a whole syn-drome of black male and female mistrust that gets passed down from mothers to sons, that affects those sons' relationships with women. Black women need not only to love their sons, they need to raise them."

I can completely identify with that. I've got two brothers, and I once said to my mom, "They're going to have a hard time like I did." She said, "Why would you say that?" And I told her, "Because we weren't taught at an early age how to be men." I was very fortunate in being involved in sports, so I got some male leadership there, but my brothers were not. Our dad left when we were tiny, and in those cases you wind up learning from the people you're around all the time, which usually isn't good. Growing up in a single-parent household means that, too damn often, black kids think it's normal to have four or five kids out of wedlock. Black girls think it's all right to get preg-nant in high school because they see it so often. My daughter said,

"Dad, what do you want from me?" I told her, "We're going to start with you going through high school not being pregnant. I know that sounds simple, but that would mean a great deal to me." Black-on-black crime, teenage pregnancy, single-parent households . . . that stuff is destroying the black family. I just think black men, overall, have done a pretty poor job in this area.

"You don't even want to get me started on the number of young women who almost compete to have babies by the least desirable man on the block—the thug, the gangster, the drug dealer," Marita said. "This is another result of our being in a spiritual malaise. We are desperately confused about who we are. Until we start listening to people like Cosby, and have more of us saying tough things, we're going to continue to be confused. The thing that's so appalling, so distressing, is that we have the access to solutions in our community. If we wanted to start a black church, do you know we could go to any bank in this region and get a loan just like that? But the churches are not necessarily dedicated to saving our people. They're dedicated to saving souls, and that's a different thing. I think that the black church is, on the one hand, doing some very progressive things, but much of the black church has become very conservative over the issue of homosexuality. There's more concern in the black church today over homosexuality than AIDS."

I almost got into a fistfight with two preachers during a meeting about support for John Kerry before the 2004 presidential election. They asked me, "Do you support homosexuality?" I said the issue here isn't homosexuality, it's more important than that, and only God can judge people. I told them that's what scares me about the religious

**agenda in this country right now. Religious people, in my mind, ought
to be compassionate and accepting toward other people. And what was
their response? "If you're with us, you're with us; if you're not, you're
not." Of all the issues people have and need to have addressed by the
black church, when did attacking homosexuality go to the top
of them?**

"I think you can trace some of that to the Republican Party making a concerted effort to reach out to the black church," Marita said.
"And it succeeded. The black church has embraced some of that
agenda. But I don't want to turn things over to the church. We can
save ourselves. We can save our kids, but only if we ourselves change.

"Here's an example of how values are so upside down. In Mitchellville, Maryland, one of the premier black suburbs in America, in our
school system we've got kids sitting in trailers because the schools are
overcrowded the minute they're constructed. So these people in half-
million-dollar homes, do you know what they are primarily concerned
about, really mad about? 'We don't have a Nordstrom's. We don't
have a Macy's.' They will picket because we don't have a Nordstrom's
and a Macy's, but when you go to a PTA meeting and talk about the
situation with our schools, they're not concerned. Remember, these
are among our best and brightest. These are the people who work in
the District of Columbia, the nation's capital, many in high-level government jobs. But when they come home, what are they worried
about? Not that their child is sitting in a trailer. Not that their child
is given a standardized test as opposed to real knowledge. They're
mad because there's no Nordstrom's.

"All praise to the young multimillionaires in our community who
are making huge amounts of money in the recording industry. But

is that going to save us? I don't think it is. That's one of the things hypnotizing our kids. And I'm going to say it right now: Too many black intellectuals are getting ensnared in the hip-hop, go-after-the-money-and-fame syndrome. We're too deep in the I-want-to-get-paid-now mode that prevents us from looking forward to the future. You might say, 'Well, Cosby's a millionaire; he can afford to say what he said.' But Martin Luther King wasn't a millionaire. Rosa Parks wasn't a millionaire."

One of the reasons I wanted to write this book was to reach out to people in the generations younger than I am, hopefully to spark a conversation among them and not just older adults. Any successful dialogue ought to benefit them because these issues are complex and there's no one answer, whether we're as diverse as some think or whether we still have some important common issues, as Marita argues. I think the one thing that is obvious is these problems, whether they're unique to black life or not, have to be addressed and probably in a public way. And if some people are uncomfortable with that kind of examination, well, maybe that's exactly the place we need to start.

THE COLOR
OF POWER
PETER
GUBER

I'm a movie-a-holic. I love the
movies. Some days I'll watch three
or four movies on satellite or DVD.
I watch good movies, bad movies,
action themes, chick flicks. I've al-
ways watched movies. And sometimes the movies infuriate me. A
whole lot of black people will tell you that, and I suspect Hispanics
and Asians often feel the same way, because we feel we are portrayed
by major films and filmmakers to be stupid, lazy, one-dimensional.
Did I miss a stereotype in there anywhere? We can be comedians, but
never characters in a responsible drama. We can be oversexed, but
never in real relationships. We can be caricatures, but not smart characters. And it gets tiring, real tiring.

So I set out to talk to a major film producer, actually a major white film producer. I was looking for a conversation with somebody who had produced major box-office hits and could tell me how race affects the film industry. So Wilbon and I sat with Peter Guber at his home in Los Angeles one Saturday morning to talk.

Peter has been not just a major player but a Hollywood force for years and years, going back to the early 1970s when he was studio chief of Columbia Pictures, into the 1970s when he founded Casablanca Records and Filmworks and had such stars as Donna Summer, Parliament and George Clinton, and the Village People, into the late 1980s when he was chairman and CEO of Sony Pictures. It was there he made *Boyz 'N the Hood* a reality. He's now the chairman and CEO of Mandalay Entertainment and host of his own television show.

Most black people who are filmgoers became familiar with his name in 1985 when he acquired the novel *The Color Purple* from Alice Walker and, with Quincy Jones as his producer, made one of the most famous films ever with a predominantly black cast, and a glamorous one at that because it included Oprah Winfrey, Danny Glover, and Whoopi Goldberg and was directed by Steven Spielberg. It became a blockbuster, and a poster of the movie sits above a fireplace in Guber's estate.

But that's not the only movie he made with cultural relevance or with people of color. There was *D.C. Cab*, which starred Mr. T, Irene Cara, and Marsha Warfield, and *Flashdance*, which made stars of Jennifer Beals and Irene Cara.

I had a lot of questions about why so few movie executives include people of color in their films and whether this is changing. About his own motives for making certain pictures. About the economic viability of films that include blacks and Hispanics. And the place to start,

obviously, was why he had a conscience about these things in the first place.

"Yeah, I've made a lot of pictures that had real social and cultural strength," Peter said. "Whether it was *Boyz 'N the Hood, Gorillas in the Mist, Midnight Express, Missing,* or *The Color Purple.* I've produced many, many films in all areas. And while I've thought those and other movies are really worthwhile and valuable, if I thought it couldn't be successful as a business proposition, I wouldn't have embraced it. I honestly believe that. I don't see myself in the proselytizing business; I see myself in the movie business, which means I had to make an artistic adventure that was an economic reality. Otherwise I'm out of business.

"It's in my self-interest, you know? People have said to me, 'Well, you have a larger view of the world and you're really spiritually centered and someone who embraces cross-cultural forces.' That's nice, and I'd like to think that all that's true. I'd love to think it. But you know what I really believe? Being inclusive has been in my self-interest. I think that it was in my self-interest, my economic interest, my family's best interests. And I don't mean that in a rude or crude way.

"When I convinced Alice Walker to give me the rights to *The Color Purple,* I completely believed in the story, but I was a middle-aged white guy and I immediately recognized that I was not the right focal point for it. And there were—you're going to be shocked—a lot of African American men who were not happy with me making that picture. Not because I was white. It was because they felt the story was anti–African American male. So I went to Quincy Jones. If you're talking about getting that project done and doing it justice, that was economic reality. It was economic and creative survival. It was community interest.

"I'd like to think that I am open and that I embrace cross-cultural forces. But if you're asking me to point to the real reasons, there's a hard reality that exists. I believe that the economic engine as it relates to a specific industry helps change people's views because it taps into their survival. If you examine why Adolph Rupp, who was a complete racist, changed his view of recruiting black athletes to the University of Kentucky, it was because he saw he couldn't win without changing his view. He couldn't survive. If you ask the movie business why it's having to change its view somewhat—there still are not a lot of African Americans or Hispanics in executive ranks, but there are a lot of women, more women than men as a matter of fact—it's because the industry finally recognized who goes to the movies. It's not out of some great kindness or change in social philosophy; it's because the industry, in order to be where it wants to be economically, had to acknowledge blacks and Hispanics are great consumers of their product. They're a terrific audience, a terrific market. And we had to tap into it.

"It's true across the spectrum. I believe sports is entertainment. I know there's athletic excellence. But when I watch a game—let's say I'm watching Charles's show on Turner—it's not just for the athletic excellence. Every piece of information is available in that telecast: scores, highlights, standings, analysis—right? I watch it because it's entertaining. It's about being entertained. It's about being consumed. You're a consumer, and you're consumed by the entertainment, you're engaged by the entertainment. The information is not even memo-

rable. I don't know who won or lost an hour afterward. But you remember the experience. You remember how you related to it.

"I know one thing absolutely for sure, that if it's different, if it
speaks a different language, if it's taller, if it comes from a different
geographic area, if it obeys a different system—we're frightened. First
thing is flight or fight. It isn't curiosity. The first response is to be critical rather than curious. I think it's in our nature. It's how all of us
are wired. What we try to overcome with part of our brain and our
consciousness is that it's *not* correct. But unfortunately, when that veneer is scratched, when you're threatened or you're frightened, you
revert to that survival mechanism."

**Even if Peter said he didn't make movies in any conscious way to
bring about social change, I wondered how he felt about their effect
on people. Did he think people can learn to be less racist by watching certain kinds of movies?**

"Relating to other people is one of those ways that we break down
tribalism," he said. "You may call it racism; I call it tribalism. Because
I'm engaged with you, because you tap into me—not intellectually but
in the heart and the gut—by what you say, by your body language, by
your involvement, by your thoughts, you know, that's what happens.
And then I'll think about it, and then I see you differently. I mean,
you personally: I'll see you differently. And that's what happens in
film, in television, in movies. It operates in a visceral sense, so over a
long period of time, if we represent cultural differences, geographic
differences, racial differences, age differences, it helps to break down
racism or tribalism. I go to an NBA game and I notice that the audi-

ence, predominantly white, is looking at a game featuring players who are eighty percent black. African Americans go to a movie theater, they see, say, *Jaws* even though there are no African Americans in it, and they love it. Relating to entertainment can help us get over our tribalism.

"I don't know that I'm driven by higher values about film or storytelling, but I do know this: People have often said to me that movies are a beacon, and they change views and enlarge the spectrum of ideas in a society. It can be movies, television, media. But I think movies mostly reflect society. Not that the other forms of media aren't somewhat of a beacon, and not that they don't have impact. They do have impact. If you look at the media of a society, you can tell so much about it. Is there anything more toxic than the eleven o'clock news? You take two sucks on the back of a car exhaust pipe, eat a pepperoni pizza, and go to sleep, and you'll be better off than watching the nightly news. The news is just corrosive. It's just terrible. And much of the time it's programming just masquerading as news. So much of it is entertainment. You know, baby falls out of window, tune in at eleven. Man kills fourteen people at school in Czechoslovakia. I mean, when does it matter—we have six billion people on the planet—that in Czechoslovakia this happened? I mean, it just doesn't relate.

"We've made a lot of progress in one way regarding race in the movies. Early on, by making the villain different—African American, Indian, Chinese, Asian—audiences could automatically spot the villain in the movie. It was easy, you know? You remember that from movies we saw growing up. Then, you got to kill the villain in the end, which meant you were safe, you were protected, and that reflected your society. But now, one of the things that is incrementally changing film is that, for economic reasons, film and television executives have to say to themselves, 'We can't do that. We can't make that group the villain all the time. (a) We'll lose the African American or Hispanic audience. (b) The government won't let us do it. And (c) most important, it's good business not to keep doing it because we want those folks.' So they begin to think of it differently. 'Let's switch the villain around.' Those are the slow, tiny accretions that happen.

"Remember, we're only a second out of 1960, only a second. I think what we have to be is completely impatient in the process. We cannot sacrifice another generation or a group of kids. You've got to be completely impatient and bring certain forces to bear. At the same time, we can't be imprudent; we have to recognize that the process will take a long time to bake in so that it's automatic, so that it's on automatic pilot. It has to get to the point where it's like driving home. You wind up thinking, 'How the hell did I get home? I don't remember driving home; the car must have driven automatically.' It's just baked into you, right? You don't have to remember putting your foot on the gas pedal or on the brake or the people walking across the street, but you wind up at home nonetheless. That's what has to happen for us to get home in the larger sense.

"For several days after 9/11 we saw the best in everybody. And you know why? I know people find this hard to believe, but it was fear."

Too often fear has been used to keep us apart. It's the fear of the unknown. That's what segregation created and built up over time. We spent so much time hating each other that we never stopped to realize that most black people and white people just want the same things in life.

Now that we're no longer legally separated by race, we're separated by money. So we still don't live together; we still don't get to see the best qualities we each have to offer.

When people watch television every night, they see the news lead off with three or four black guys who committed a crime or did something stupid. Or they watch sports and see some loudmouth black guy like Terrell Owens. Or Allen Iverson's late to practice again. There are so many negative images that you see. You don't see the good things black people are doing for themselves, for their communities. And you never see stories of white people doing things to help blacks.

They don't know if they can trust us; we don't know if we can trust them. The system teaches you not to trust other people. We don't live together, so our images are from television and newspapers. The people—black people, white people, poor people—have to band together and say our enemy is the system. That's the problem.

It's not working for poor whites. There are more poor white people than there are poor black people. In fact, white people make up almost half of the people living in poverty in the United States. And yet they're against blacks as if it's their fault when almost a quarter of all black people are living in poverty themselves. They don't understand we have to work together. This hasn't been going on for a week. It's been going on for four hundred years of races being pitted against one another.

"I faced tribalism when I grew up," Peter Guber said. "I was beaten up in school. I experienced it. So I understand, although other people experience it more pervasively, more continuously. But I have seen changes in my sixty years of being alive. I've seen changes that

I think are material. But I've seen them in only two areas that are really the important forces: the reality of economics, and government laws that provide the stick. Those two things over a long enough period of time will be reflected in films, in entertainment, music, and all kinds of things. And they'll be ingested into the system.

"I gave Nelson Mandela his seventieth birthday event when he came to the United States. And I kept thinking to myself, Why did this guy call me? Why me? Why not Quincy Jones or Sidney Poitier? Why me? He called David Rockefeller on the East Coast, and he called me out here. So when I was having lunch with him, I said, 'Mr. Mandela, how come you called me to do this?' And he said, 'Because you were in power and you can help assemble the right people and you could help accomplish what I needed to accomplish.' He was very practical. He used the forces he could to get a result. That's real. He didn't call some poor and out-of-work fellow down in south Los Angeles. No, he looked where there were buttons to push and pushed the right buttons to get what he wanted.

"Now I do see more inclusiveness among young people. I look at it in my business culturally, that African Americans in fashion and music, sports and entertainment, are the trendsetters. They're not just there; they're the trendsetters. You see it across the whole spectrum. You're seeing a different racial culture that's in America today. Not exponentially different, but a little different.

"I really believe film and television are a fairly accurate reflection of where we are. I believe that films and entertainment have to provide nourishment to a society. It can be very inspirational, absolutely. But you know, if you get too far away from reality—from certainty, you have too much variety, you drive too far in the other direction, nobody comes. It's got to be just enough, got to move it, got to create it, and I think we're doing that.

"But I worry, candidly, I worry that government and the economy, the two major forces holding things together, are fragile. The government's fragile and the economic engine's fragile. If you get a lot of people out of work and get real hard times, you'll get a government in a different posture and you see tribalism emerging again. That's what I worry about. And who can wait a thousand years? We're only here for a short period of time. Look at the dinosaurs and the sharks and the other creatures on this planet. Long periods. And we've been here [slaps the table] like that. An instant in time.

"These are very complex issues. They defy easy, simplistic solutions. It has to be comprehensive. It has to be educational; it has to be environmental and cultural. The culture has to support it through its laws. The economic engine has to be strong enough to reward those who behave that way. That's what we have to look at. I think films and entertainment have done it better than most businesses. You look in front of the camera, at performance, and there's plenty of color. I mean the best. It's even more noticeable in the sports fields. But when you look into the executive ranks, you have a far smaller group, and if you look at women of color, you have an even smaller group. That's true about Asians and Hispanics, too. It's not just true about African Americans. I think it's tribalism at work. We, as a tribe, walk around and tend to be more comfortable around people who speak our language, who look like us and have had some common experiences, come from the same geographic areas.

"My metaphor is this: You've got a big vat of vanilla ice cream. Put one little drop of purple dye in it, mix that all up, and nothing happens. Put another drop of purple dye in; nothing happens. You do that 500 times and nothing happens. On the 506th time, the whole thing turns purple. Do you know when it will turn? Nobody really knows, so that's the problem. You've got to be one of those drops.

"I could be pretentious and say, 'Well, it's better in film now and I'm very optimistic.' And yes, I see what certain projects are doing economically. But still, there's just one or two, maybe three drops of purple dye in that vanilla ice cream. How many will it take? You got to be committed that you'll do it, and you'll stay the course as long as it takes, and pray to God that ice cream doesn't go out of fashion before the thing changes."

As we talked with Peter Guber, I wondered what films he might be working on now or what he might be planning for the future.

"As you get older you've got less time," he said, "so you want to do more things because you realize time is so precious. I've done thirty-four years' worth of films. I've overseen a thousand movies at three giant studios, been the corporate head, produced fifty-five movies, four times for best picture. Now I don't want to do more; I want to do different.

"I want to try to do a film that hasn't been done about Frank Sinatra," Peter continued. "He was truly Jekyll and Hyde. This guy, if not bipolar, was very dark. He had two different personalities. I met him many times, six, seven different times on business, and he was a scary guy, a force of nature. Then he would walk out onstage and sing. And where did that sound come from? That's one film I'd like to do.

"I also want to do a film about the history of rap, not the whole history of rap, but the idea of how this culture emerged, and to find the right characters for it. What was the synthesis? Is it the language of that tribe? Is it a force of society? James Baldwin once said to me, 'Each age and each culture has moments where its poetry, its language, says something about the larger issue. And if you can find them and you can mine them, you can tap into them, you can move them across all kinds of media.' Television, movies, whatever. You have to find the sound, the language. You know, like Bob Dylan had a sound, and he just kind of moved across them. Ray Charles had a sound. And there's something about rap that strikes me. I was a complete rock-and-roller; I loved hard rock, loved it, loved it. And my folks hated it. They called it the devil. Now with rap, my kids are so into it, and I couldn't get my arms around it. First, I was threatened: 'Shut it off! It's too damn noisy! I don't know what they're saying! What are they talking about?' Then I became curious; maybe it was just that one drop of purpose in me that said, 'Be curious and not so critical.' I began to listen and came to recognize that it's the poetry of a generation. It's not just the melody, it's the lyrics . . . really the combination of the two. From that curiosity I became interested. And from that interest I became passionate to see if I could find a way to express that. You know, I never admitted it for two years to my kids.

"One of the ironies of storytelling is the human psyche struggles with two forces. Audiences want certainty, yet they want variety. The conundrum is that they're opposite. People say, 'I want to be certain when I go to a movie that I'm going to like it. I want to be certain that I'm going to see stars. And I want to know the story.' So in trying to be different, you want the story to be ten percent different, perhaps twelve percent different. You don't want it to be a hundred eighty percent different. It's navigating that space that is maybe fifteen or twenty degrees off of what was done that is the sweet spot. It's the place to aim.

"I'm a storyteller. My legacy is storytelling. You know, we're all from the same base. A very small tribe of humans emerged from Africa and populated the world. So everybody's connected. You have to be a complete idiot to think 'My God's better than your God.' It's just insane. But what kept the tribes working was the ritual of sameness. There's this survival mechanism—primal brain—that said that anything that's different from me is something I have to fear. And f-e-a-r is nothing but 'false evidence appearing real.' It appears real. It's different. It's a different color, different religion, different language. Anything that differentiated us made us, at first, frightening. It made us move away. As an animal—I mean a primal animal, part of the animal kingdom—we see this throughout all species, so we're not different from that but what we've done is lay on a cultural veneer to try to recognize that it's not real. It's false evidence appearing real. It's not real.

"What worries me is what's going on in the world today, all over the world, not just what's black or white or black vs. white. It's Protestant against Catholic. It's Arab against Israeli, Jew against Christian, the Muslim view against the Judeo-Christian view. These are all very powerful engines. They tap into our primitive self and so what we do is our mammalian brain, our more intellectual self, our cerebral cortex saying, 'Wait a minute, that's ridiculous, that's false evidence appearing real. I'm—we're—better than that, and we need each other to survive because we can't survive individually.'"

THE COLOR OF POWER   165

It's clear, for whatever reason, that Peter hasn't let fear dominate his agenda. Survival plays a part in everybody's decision making. But the problem I have is that since Peter has been so phenomenally successful—controversial yes, he has had and has now his feuds and disputes with other major players in the industry—why haven't others seen that being inclusive, expansive, creative can benefit them economically as well? How come some other studio executives don't want to make money off the black moviegoing public and therefore expand the opportunities of black and Hispanic actors, directors, writers? Peter talks about fear, and it's fair to wonder—though nobody who is afraid will ever give you a candid answer—just how afraid some of his peers are.

"Yes, fear can overwhelm the inclination to comply or to do something because it's good business," Peter said. "It's Adolph Rupp standing in the hallway after they lost to West Texas, saying to himself, 'Hmmm. If I wanna stay here, I'd better make this change,' but at the same time wrestling with, 'I may not like it. I may not feel good about it,' then going back and forth until he said, 'But I'm going to do it, all right?' Some people can't. They give in to their worst fears.

"Howard Shultz [CEO of Starbucks] saw it was good business to go into urban communities and partner up with Earvin [Magic Johnson]. For him, it was 'I see that it's good business, all right? And I like and respect this particular man.' I'm saying that it's the two pieces together: recognizing that if a company—and I'm talking now in general and not about Starbucks, which is a great example of what works—doesn't make these kinds of moves, government and society might look at you negatively and it might affect your economic engine. I know it's crude to say it, but I believe those two pieces have to work together and over a long, long period of time to rewire us.

"Why do I think it's necessary? There's so much mobility in the planet now. There are so many people interfacing. There's so much intermarriage and cultural diversity and so many things happening that over time there's a new engine. When I grew up in the fifties, you didn't know a bus turned over in Korea, or that somebody was fighting in Armenia till four months after it happened. Now, somebody burps in Yugoslavia or there's an argument in Colombia or there's a drama in Detroit, instantaneously it's there in your face. So we're connected in a unique way. Nobody is alone anymore. We're always connected. So that's going to be another push in favor of rewiring, trying to push past tribalism.

"I saw this incredible documentary years ago on the Ku Klux Klan and it stuck with me forever. It showed three-, four-, five-, six-year-old kids who were bred to hate. They were standing there with Klan members saying, 'I don't like Catholics. I don't like blacks. I don't like Jews.' And of course they had no idea what a Catholic or Jew was. Or what being black even meant. So you have to think to yourself that's been inculcated as part of that tribe into them. It's a long, relentless road that has to overcome a lot of history baked into our brain, baked into our society . . . so that ultimately you'll have a more compassionate world that isn't built on those tribal differences. It may still be built on economic differences. It'll always be built on self-interest. It'll always be built on survival, but the survival will recognize a different paradigm and say, 'We all have to survive for any of us to survive.' You can't be rich and have everything while people around you are not eating. Once you begin to recognize that, you realize that you have to change some of those values and beliefs.

"I remember the first time I went to Sri Lanka. It was a thirty-hour flight, and it turned into the most incredible experience I ever had. I went out in the morning early, and every single person in the entire giant city was of color. Every single person. There wasn't one white person but me. After about three minutes or four minutes, I got nervous. And I thought to myself, 'Why am I nervous? No one will bother me. Why am I nervous?' Then, after I pulled myself together I thought, 'I wonder if that's what an African American person feels like when they walk into a big white community?' I was bringing all of my own prejudices, all of my own fears, all of my own survival instincts into that experience. It was false evidence appearing real. I felt, 'Oh my God, someone's going to do something to me because they're a different tribe, they're Indian!' I'm a highly educated person. I have four degrees. I've had every cultural experience imaginable. I've traveled extensively. But pardon the expression, the devil lives inside of me in that context. The demon lives in me, and I have to stand guard in the portals of my mind all the time. Not my heart, my mind. I have to say to myself—we all do—'Wait a minute now, where am I coming from?' "

To me, the solution is so easy, but the task is so difficult. It's like losing weight: You've got to burn more than you eat. It sounds simple, but it's really hard. It's the same with racism. And just like it's hard to keep your mind off eating when you're constantly seeing delicious food on television, the constant negative images we see of each other make it a struggle to do the right thing. *I saw this black guy killing people on TV, so how can I trust them? I just saw this white guy stealing money; why should I trust them?* There are so many underlying messages you get, knocking you off the real path.

Peter Guber realized that you don't always have to show the bad side of people. Initially, he caught me off guard when he said he didn't make these movies to be nice, he did it to make money. But it's understandable when you think about it.

Economics has to be the stick that drives us back together. Why not be up-front about it? When a white person tries to help, people say, "There's got to be an angle." Same thing with black people. If there's money for the taking, it doesn't matter where it's coming from. Make sure you get a piece of it.

Rich people are always going to be rich. They have their own game going. They have their own schools, their own neighborhoods. And if you try to go to their neighborhoods, you'll be arrested. Poor people have to realize they need each other to survive.

And you look at where the priorities are. The public school system for our poor people is the worst in the industrialized world, and we just let it go, say we don't have the money to improve it.

Then, when the tsunami hit Southeast Asia at the end of 2004, the government and the private sector came up with a billion dollars in aid. All of our schools and poor neighborhoods are being run into the ground; we're laying off police officers and firefighters. And when one bad thing happens, we come up with a billion dollars? Didn't they just tell us they didn't have any money? That just shows the money is there, but they're not sharing it with the people who need it on a daily basis. The reason is because it doesn't affect their own kids.

I was impressed with Peter Guber because he understood that for Hollywood power brokers, it's a game. They don't care one way or the other.

As he said, the movies have been perpetuating these myths for a long time. The Indian's the bad guy, blacks are bad guys, and now the Muslim's the bad guy. Of course, America's going to think that when that's all they see.

I don't know if it's guilt or whatever, but Peter Guber's trying to do some good stuff. It took some guts to do *The Color People*. And he didn't say, "I'm trying to be this great person." He said, "I'm trying to make money, and I figured out how to do that while doing the right thing." I respect him for that.

CARRYING
IT FORWARD
JESSE
JACKSON

We didn't know, when we reached Reverend Jesse Jackson's office, that he was preparing to celebrate his sixty-third birthday. It's easy to forget how long Reverend Jackson has been a figure of national prominence and significance. Inside his headquarters in the Hyde Park section of the South Side of Chicago are photos so historically significant, the building pretty much feels like a museum. There are photos of Reverend Jackson at the front of famous marches, of him huddled with Dr. King, with Reverend Ralph Abernathy. Nearly forty-five years of history fill that office and shape who he is and what he is still about. A trip down memory lane with Jesse Jackson is like a time line of the civil rights movement.

"I was jailed July 17, 1960, trying to use a public library in Greenville, South Carolina," Reverend Jackson said. "Jailed again in '62, '63. Came to grad school in '64. Was in the Selma march for the right to vote in '65. And that's when I started working for Dr. King, in '65. We had a summer camp here in '66, that's when I started Operation Breadbasket, working with people.

"And we've been having a weekly meeting every Saturday since that time. When I started here in '66, we didn't have any black check-out clerks at grocery stores. Blacks couldn't drive milk trucks. Couldn't drive garbage trucks, not in '66. I had the choice a few years earlier of trying to go pro in baseball or going on to college. I'm so glad I chose college, though it was a difficult choice for a while because I loved baseball so much. Still, my father was militant on the subject. Big Boss said, 'It is clear to me that the risk of going to a baseball system versus a college education is not a good trade-off.' "

Because Jesse ran for president, and because he's been involved in Democratic Party politics for more than twenty years, I'm not sure people under thirty-five think of him as anything but a politician. I don't think people realize he is one of the last really prominent links to the civil rights movement. I don't think people realize he's a scholar. I know I'd forgotten how brilliant the man is, and how passionate he is. And he's wound up these days—I don't think he would mind me saying that. He's wound up because he doesn't see people knowing about their own culture, their own religion, their race. He doesn't see young people, especially the young black people he's trying to reach, understanding their connection to the entire world and how they fit in it—not like other people around the world do.

"There's no context when most of us discuss racial issues," Reverend Jackson told us. "When Jews have a seder once a year and close down everything, it means that every year they discuss seven thousand years of history. Not just last year. They go back to Abraham. Their history is *spoken*.

"We black people don't have the sense, for the most part, that slavery was the law of the land until 1865, for 246 years. That's why institutions, some of this country's most historically significant institutions, reflect those 246 years—like Brown, Harvard, Yale. Their founders and officers were shippers and slave traders. I think Yale has twelve colleges and something like eleven of them are named after people who were either slave traders or shippers of our people. We don't have that discussion. Or that there were something like 79,000 lynchings between that time and the year 2000. Lynchings took place on Sunday afternoon after church. You'd see people going to church. Everybody saw it. They grew into our psyche: We were less than poor people. The Supreme Court looked at it and was fine with Jim Crow segregation. Jim Crow was a Supreme Court ruling. And it took us until 1954 to be rid of it. So from 1619 until 1954, that's 335 years of legalized racial supremacy. The law of the land. The *law*. And even when we were legally guaranteed the right to vote in '65, they used schemes to undermine the impact of it. It took another twenty-five years to begin to get representatives.

"People ask me, 'Jesse, do you celebrate July 4?' And I ask, 'Which July 4? July 4, 1776?' We were already 157 years into slavery then. Black people were totally ignored as it related to freedom. There wasn't any mention of us. Whites won freedom from Britain, but we didn't win freedom from slavery. So I say July 4, 1776, is of limited meaning for us except to say that it was when whites who came to America declared their independence from Britain."

Even though Reverend Jackson has been interviewed and written about for forty years, a lot of people still don't know that sports wasn't an interest he adopted only in adult life. He really could have played professional baseball. The Chicago White Sox, among others, scouted him. A whole lot of his research is sports-based, whether it's dealing with graduation rates or the numbers of minority candidates hired or interviewed in the major team sports in America. And because of his intimate involvement with sports, Reverend Jackson is quick to see how advancement for people of color in America often comes in sports years before such inclusion reaches black folks who are not involved in athletics. This isn't an isolated fact, he stressed:

"In slavery, the weak were left behind. Those who were strong became championship cotton pickers, Olympic cotton pickers. They became plantation stars, superstar cotton pickers. 'I can pick forty pounds a day,' they'd say. What was bad was we could pick the cotton, but we could not gin it and sell it in the market. We could pick the cotton, but we couldn't turn it into textiles. It was a pattern that was set, even for the most accomplished black men.

"Jack Johnson's boxing victory in 1910 was a huge breakthrough, psychologically, for black people," Reverend Jackson said. "It's hard to imagine what Jack Johnson, as a fighter of such renown, meant to people who couldn't vote, who couldn't teach in the public schools, who couldn't work downtown in stores or shops. But with Johnson, that 'inferior' Negro beat a 'superior' white man. And then he took up with a white woman. People in America went crazy on Jack Johnson. He had to get out of here, had to get out of the country and go to Canada. White folks wouldn't let another black man fight for the heavyweight title until Joe Louis.

"Jack Johnson was a hero by necessity. So was Jesse Owens. Here comes the 1936 Olympics, with Hitler wrapped up in the notion of Aryan superiority, and Americans didn't have anybody else who could outrun the German sprinters. So it was left to Jesse Owens to beat the German sprinters on the road, in Berlin. Of course, as big as the Olympics were, as big as track and field was then, it wasn't the same as being the heavyweight champion of the world. Hitler had one more person, he thought: Max Schmeling. And while he won the first fight, Joe Louis came back in ninety-seven seconds in the second fight. Took his ribs out. Cracked them. People could hear them crack at ringside. And of course, he was champion for the next thirteen years. It's hard to imagine what a necessary hero Joe Louis was. My name is Jesse Louis Jackson. A lot of kids were named after the Brown Bomber back in 1940."

Today we don't have what Reverend Jackson called "heroes by necessity." It's impossible for people under, say, sixty years of age to imagine how rare it was to see Joe Louis win a fight or Jesse Owens win a race. But it's through Joe Louis and Jesse Owens, once they were allowed to compete, that folks back home could see what was possible with opportunity, that no amount of bigotry mattered in a fair competition.

"What makes black folks so successful in football and baseball and basketball and track?" Reverend Jackson asked. "Why are we the best in the world at so many of those world events? Arguably, three rea-sons. One, the playing field is even. Whether we're talking about picking cotton, prize fighting, shooting a basketball, or hitting .300 on a baseball diamond, whenever there is one set of rules, we can be champions no matter what the odds against us are. Two, the rules are public. And three, the criteria are clear. That football field is 55 yards wide, 100 yards long, 10 yards for all first downs. Whenever the field is even, we can just be supreme. On a basketball court, when you shoot and that ball goes through that hoop, everybody knows it went through. Now, choosing the next president of the University of Iowa or University of Michigan, that is a closed-door decision. A director-ship or executive position at the county hospital, the physicians have a meeting and say 'Let's discuss this.' The rules certainly aren't pub-lic. There might not even be any rules. We cannot win when decisions are subjective, when they're made behind closed doors. Sometimes the criteria seem to shift.

"We have figured out, in the field of play, how to maneuver as long as the criteria don't shift. Even before 1947, we were able to play baseball. Ted Williams, Joe DiMaggio, Babe Ruth in the twenties and thirties—those guys knew blacks could play baseball from exhibition tours. Ability was not the issue. Legal race supremacy was the issue. There were the barnstorming tours. Hardly any of the players were making more than $5,000 a year. So the season's over, they would take these tours across the South. Satchel Paige and his All-Stars would draw as many people in the South as white stars.

"I maintain there was no legitimate major league until 1947. Be-fore that there was a black league and a white league. It became major to me when they could both play together, but not until everybody could play. We didn't know how good baseball was until everybody could play. We didn't know how good Ted Williams was, how good Satchel Paige was, how good any of them were until they played against the best of the best, regardless of color. That kind of racism hurt the white players, too. It deprived them of the chance to play with and against the best players of that time.

"The NBA had something similar going on. Marques Haynes could play. But he couldn't play initially in a white market. He was kept separate and could play for the Harlem Globetrotters. The Minneapolis Lakers were called World Champion Lakers. But what they were was White Champions. The Harlem Globetrotters beat them in Chicago twice. Before long came the idea that maybe it's time to let blacks in the NBA.

"One of the reasons athletics are so important is because they're objective. The rules are clear. It's the place in our culture where people are most likely to have the chance to prove they can compete. Subjectivity doesn't come into play. Either you can win the game or you can't. Ability didn't change. The law changed. The right to vote changed. Nothing changed but the law. And so out of this comes Jackie Robinson. Then, on opening day, 1972, the twenty-fifth anniversary of his first playing, people said, 'Jackie, isn't this great?' He said, 'It won't be great until blacks can at least be third-base coach.' Twenty-five years later and there's still no black third-base coach.

"Athletes have a special gift. David was an athlete. David smoked Goliath. It's a big deal. Great athletes are given many gifts: physical, emotional, psychological. There's the gift of charisma. Charles, you didn't just decide to be this height. You didn't decide to be able to do what you could do."

The struggle just to be included went on for fifty years. The entry of black players led to pushing for more managers and coaches. I think the NBA has progressed to the point where it's no longer news when a black coach is hired or fired. It's no different from the white coaches, which was the point all along. That said, how many of the really good jobs—on the teams with talented, playoff-tested veterans—go to black coaches? Only four black coaches have ever won championships in the NBA, and none since K. C. Jones did it with the Boston Celtics in 1986. So there's still that glass ceiling.

It's better than football. At the end of 2004 there were only three black head coaches among the 117 major college football teams.

How many times have we had this argument? It seems like it comes up every two years. I'm sick of bitching about it. What's even more depressing is how low the bar is to appease us. We stopped talking about it for a couple of years because we had five black coaches. *Five.* It was like "We've really made it now." That's what's scary about it. Those were considered the good ol' days.

How are we supposed to make progress on the heavy issues, like fixing our schools, when we can't even get a couple more coaches hired? We spend so much time talking about this. We're fighting so many battles on so many fronts.

In this case, we aren't marching through the streets or staging the lunch-counter sit-ins like those in the 1960s that led to basic deseg-regation, and then to fuller inclusion in any part of American life. But sports is probably, for better or worse, the place in American life where we are still more likely to be able to see just how black partic-ipation can work.

"We have to be aware of something larger than playing," Reverend Jackson told us. "Even Michael Jordan found that out the hard way. He was reminded that if the rules weren't public he didn't have the same chance as when they were, when he was playing the game. The criteria weren't clear for Michael when it came to Abe Pollin deciding who would run his basketball franchise, now was it? He fires him, and when Michael says, 'I'd like to know why,' Pollin says, 'I don't owe you nothing.' That's cold, man. Do you know how cold that was? I mean, this is Michael. He has to be thinking, 'You owe me nothing? I gave you two years and filled every seat in your building, filled every stadium where your team played for you. I did two years virtually for free.' Doesn't get much colder than that. Michael entertained. He made a franchise. But he got run out of there. So the struggle's not over.

"We must be intelligent about it because the part that's clearly defined, the physical part, doesn't last that long. You have these five to ten years of glory that are down payments for the rest of your life. It's just a ten-year down payment on the rest of your life. Guys are thinking, 'I'm free to do whatever I want to.' Free? You ain't free. You're free to get cut. You're free to be undercut while driving to the basket or trying to throw a block and get your career shortened. You're free to have a car wreck. You're free, if you're in the NFL, to have a contract conditioned upon performance. This is why once a year I look at the top sixty-four college basketball programs and forty of them haven't graduated a ballplayer in ten years.

"Free? We've gone from picking cotton balls to picking footballs, basketballs, and baseballs. There was nothing really wrong with picking cotton balls, except that we could not grow a textile industry. And there's nothing wrong with picking footballs, basketballs, and baseballs except that we don't share in the running of the multibillion-dollar industry that is sports, whether it's ownership or televising the games or working as the athletic director or running the arena or examining the players. Everything beyond the field or the court is an issue, usually a race issue. But there's all the evidence in the world that the kids who compete now have no idea of how much sacrifice was undertaken, how much groundwork was laid."

I'm not sure it's fair to compare life on campus to life on the plantation. If you get to college, that at least gives you a chance to be successful. You're where everything's happening. You're not in the ghetto, you're not in the country, you're not in the 'hood. You're at an institute of higher learning. You at least have a chance to be successful.

The big problem I have with these colleges is that they're not taking care of these kids and making sure they're graduating, or even getting an education. A major burden is on these colleges. The kids aren't supposed to be in college for the schools to get four years of basketball or football out of them and then wave good-bye. They're supposed to be in college to learn. And you can't put all of the burden on an eighteen-year-old kid.

If you ask an eighteen-year-old if all he wants to do is play sports, he'll answer, "Hell yeah!" So they'll tell him, "If you take these hard classes, there's a chance you'll be ineligible. So we'll put you in this easy class so you can play sports."

When that happens, the college players are not learning what they need in order to succeed in the world. They're not on course to graduate, and they aren't graduating. That's the problem. A scholarship

doesn't equal an education. It just gives the university time to make money off the kids. That's all. Education is only valuable if you actually receive it.

And, of course, the first area young black athletes need to be educated in is history. Their own history.

"Jack Johnson was a big deal," Reverend Jackson reminds us. "Winning was a big deal, dating that white woman at the turn of the twentieth century was a big deal, and getting run out of the country to Canada was a big deal. Joe Louis fighting Max Schmeling was a big deal. Jesse Owens winning in front of Hitler was a big deal. Jackie Robinson's breakthrough was a big deal. In some ways, these things were bigger than what happened in entertainment. Harry Belafonte and Sammy Davis and Lena Horne could sing in places before blacks could eat in them. They'd come into these restaurants through the kitchen and leave through the kitchen. They'd have to stay at the black hotel down the street even though they were selling out the big room at the richest, whitest hotels in town. I don't mean southern hotels; I mean the biggest, richest, whitest hotels in New York City. But the talented black athletes even more than the entertainers opened doors.

"The reason the entertainers dressed the way they dressed, on the stage, was they knew they were reflecting an entire race on stage. Now, off the stage, and they never would discuss it, people were shooting up heroin and this and that. But publicly, they were representing our race. A lot of guys now feel no sense of that."

You listen to Reverend Jackson now, and it's a little like listening to Bill Cosby. They are both men in their sixties who are obviously worried about losing certain gains people fought and died for. They're worried about a disconnect, worried substance is getting kicked in the butt by style. Most of all, as Reverend Jackson said, they're worried the wealthiest folks in the black world are choosing to communicate the wrong messages. And even though I'm twenty years younger, Reverend Jackson's concerns sound a whole lot like my mother's and grandmother's concerns years and years ago about racial pride. It's not unique to us, but we know how it affects our communities, our children. My mother and grandmother always talked about pride and dignity, and that how being poor or living in the projects shouldn't ever strip you of your dignity.

When I first got in the NBA, I was still dressing like a college kid, wearing sweat suits all around town, even to the arenas. Dr. J told me, "You can wear those warm-up suits for a little bit, but then you've got to buy some suits." I was a kid from Alabama, not used to having any money, always going around in cheap stuff. But I saw the way Dr. J was dressed, the way Maurice Cheeks and Andrew Toney dressed all the time. We were all making big money. We had to dress the part.

Whenever I see injured players wearing sweat suits or jeans while sitting on the bench, it makes me want to puke. Are you kidding me? If you're injured, either stay in the locker room or put on a suit.

There's an image to uphold. For the most part, whenever you hear the word *image*, that means "How much product can we sell with you?" That's all image seems to mean. Anytime something happens, the first thing anybody says is "image." All image means is: How can we sell your face and our products?

Many players have no idea how big the business of sports and entertainment really is. White fans and sponsors are not going to pay a lot of money to see black guys act the fool. That's just a fact. When you've got guys making $10 or $20 million a year, the only way those salaries get paid is through television and advertisements. If they can't make that money back because the black guys are taking the money and not giving anything back to the game, it's going to kill the NBA. If rappers keep disrespecting the culture at large, it will stop the dollars flowing through hip-hop.

"When rappers think they are free enough to sell records to white people where they're calling each other 'Nigger,' it just kills me," Reverend Jackson said. "Lord, it hurts. Because I know how long it took white folks just to get ahold of our name. I know how long it took to be called Mister and Miss instead of 'Hey you!' Back then, dignity was a weapon. It meant that much. How we behaved. How we handled ourselves publicly. How we went about daily life, even if we were poor, even if we had no access to formal higher education. Our speakers were more eloquent then than today. Our athletes were more graceful. Dignity itself was a weapon. Others could not put us down, and we would stand tall in many cases only by the miracle of dignity. Sundays my grandma would go to work where I knew she'd make stockings. For my brother and me to have matching socks, she'd make that sacrifice. On Sundays, she'd put on her Sunday clothes 'cause she was gonna have to face the white people. She knew what the deal was. On Thanksgiving Day, we would play football down the hill with a rag wrapped around a can. We didn't have a real football, but we were fearless down there. And we would play until our mothers came home from serving white folks Thanksgiving dinner. They would cook more than the white folks could eat and they would bring us some. I never saw a turkey on our table until I was almost twenty years old. We used to have ham for Thanksgiving. We'd sit down and they'd say, 'Eat.' They'd bring us home what they couldn't fit in the refrigerator. I mean, that's our background. And even so, you walked a certain way. You had dignity even if it meant not having much to eat.

"My father came back from World War II and had to sit behind boxes on the train because the boxes were white. I remember hearing a story about soldiers returning from overseas. They came back together on a ship. They arrived in New York and were so happy to see the Statue of Liberty for the first time. They got on the train, some with their girlfriends and wives. They'd pass Baltimore, then Washington. A whole lot of them were seeing the Capitol for the very first time. They had helped win the war. They fought in some of the bloodiest battles in American history. Won the war, mind you. But none of that mattered when the train conductor said, 'We're south of Washington.' "

Reverend Jackson's eyes began to water at the telling of the story. He didn't finish the thought, but he didn't have to. The black soldiers had to change cars, go to the last car on the train . . . by law. If folks who endured all that still managed to maintain their dignity, then it's difficult for him—or me, for that matter—to understand not caring about dignity now, about having no pride in appearance or in the way they carry themselves.

"I ask these kids now why they wear their pants so low, why I can see the crevice of their asses because the pants and the shorts are so low. I say to them, 'Tell me who designed those jeans. One of y'all, tell me real quick.' And of course," he said, "nobody can tell me. And

I tell them, 'I'm going to tell you who designed them: somebody who just got out of jail. In jail, you can't wear a belt. You can't wear a belt or a rope around your waist. You just wear what they issue to you. And it doesn't fit so the pants fall down around your ass. They take the strings out of your shoes because you might try to hang yourself. So here you are, walking around with your pants down, like you can't have a belt, and your shoes without the laces, as if somebody took them away. That's jail culture. Nobody designed that. It's jail culture, that's all it is.'"

I wondered whether Reverend Jackson agreed with what Bill Cosby said, and it didn't take long to find out. I asked him what percentage of Cosby's criticism he found legitimate.

"A hundred," he said. "Bill's intent was pure. Bill's saying, 'We can't make it this way.' Bill was saying, 'You may not be responsible for being down, but you must be responsible for getting up. If you're behind, you have to run faster. You can't waste time looking at the crowd, saying, "Look, I'm behind." Nobody cares. So run faster.' Bill is saying, 'Get up, catch up. If you're behind, run faster and if you're down, get up. Shoot straighter, jump higher.' This isn't a new lesson. I'm surprised at the negative reaction directed at Bill.

"We cannot keep blaming other folks for some of what ails us. I still go to the Cook County Jail every Christmas morning. I go there about three or four times a year other than that. I remember once asking, 'How many of you went to college, at least started college?' Four, five, or six raised their hands. I asked, 'How many of you are in for nonviolent drug charges, no gun involved?' Only some of them raised a hand. 'How many of you been in jail before?' All of them raised a hand. I said, 'All right. I got a plan to get y'all out of this jail. I'm gonna close this jail down. No black college in America has the budget these jails do. Not Howard University. Not North Carolina A&T.' I said, 'I think the security guard should have a real job instead of watching you all day.'

"And they all screamed, *'Yeah!'* I asked, 'How many of y'all want to help me close the jail down?' They clapped and clapped and screamed, 'What do we do, Reverend?' And I said, 'Don't do anything that brings you back here no more.' And they said, 'Aw, shit.'

"It's that simple, though. Don't come back no more."

Reverend Jesse Jackson is still delivering the message, whether or not the audience is ready to make the commitment with him. Who out there can match his efforts, so strong for so long, in the face of so much adversity?

It's a never-ending war. Jesse's been doing it for forty years. Yes, things are better. No, all white people are not racists. But how many times do we have to have the same arguments again and again?

I wonder if young black men understand that they have something to carry on. There's an obligation. If they could sit there with Jesse Jackson, they would get it.

I was talking to the same man who was in those pictures with Martin Luther King and Muhammad Ali and Malcolm X—three of my heroes. How many people around today ever stood in the presence of all three of those men? Jesse Jackson did.

He's a common thread, a string that reaches back to the time when the people taking stands against racism had water shot at them and

dogs sicced on them. Anyone can do it now. The hardest part is over, and yet there are still those who don't want to put in the work.

The main thing I got from Jesse Jackson is that we have to carry the fight forward. Just because we have a few black guys who sing and make a ton of money for themselves or play basketball and make a ton of money for themselves, that's not what the struggle is about. The struggle is about bringing everybody else up with you.

STEP ON
THAT FIELD
ROBERT
JOHNSON

Acquiring a pro basketball franchise probably isn't the most difficult thing Bob Johnson has ever done, no ma tter how high-profile it is and no matter how many black people marvel at what it means for a black man to own an NBA team fewer than forty years after civil rights marches.

Only twenty years before purchasing the Charlotte expansion team, which was later named the Bobcats, Bob and Sheila Johnson, then his wife, who was teaching music, took out a $40,000 second mortgage on their home in northwest Washington, D.C., to start a television network. That's how Black Entertainment Television, or BET, was born. He built a television empire from nothing but a second mortgage. He's totally self-made. Americans say they like people to pull them-

selves up by their bootstraps. Well, that's what Bob Johnson did multiple times. He had to become a tough negotiator, build alliances with
people who didn't particularly want him to make it in the first place,
and satisfy a constituency and shareholders who probably had little
in common.

Yet Bob Johnson turned his business into an empire and himself
into the richest black man in America. His programming on BET may
come under criticism from those with other agendas. But how many
of those people have understood the market and its forces like Bob
has? He has been in the news more than ever since 2002 because he
acquired an NBA franchise, which is run day-to-day by another
African American, Ed Tapscott.

While the perception of Bob Johnson might have changed, it
doesn't mean his own perceptions have dramatically changed. We
talked about his personal history and his outlook on what black folks
need to do now.

"You know I was a history major in school," said Bob, "and the way
I see it is that when you look at race in America, it has always been
defined by a sense of white supremacy. You can't push a button and
eradicate it or inoculate people against it. It's always going to be
there, but once you know you have that background, what you have
to do in your own mind—and then collectively—is to ask, how do we
deal with that knowing it's there? You have to then figure out how you,
as an individual, and how we, as a group, move to overcome that.

"Throughout black life we have tried to overcome it. We have tried
to overcome it by turning inward to our own sense of religion. Slaves,
even when they were being beaten and denied reading and fundamental rights, looked for their future in heaven and in the message

from the church and from religious leaders. That's been carried over to today, where most of our traditional leaders came out of the church. And that was the way you were carried. Then as people began to migrate north from the South and people began to, in the civil rights movement, agitate for change and new laws, you saw the rise of the social activists who started focusing on race as something we have to agitate against, we got to fight against, we got to picket, we got to demonstrate, we got to march. You get everybody from Malcolm to Stokely Carmichael to Ron Dellums, all of them agitating for change. Then, from that, you see a rise in the entrepreneur: business guys who started making money on the side doing things serving the needs of black folks. John Johnson did it with *Ebony* magazine, George Johnson did it with hair care, and so on.

"When you add all of that together, here we are in 2005, where you have vestiges of all of those things. You still have a group of people who believe the way is through the church. You still have a group who believes it's through political, social agitation. You have another group who believes that we need to start looking at our own financial well-being. The problem is that none of them is going to answer it all by themselves.

"From my standpoint, my strength and my background are ignoring what the system is. Go at it, fight against it the best way you know how, which is to not let it intimidate you, and use every asset that you have to achieve your own objective and not worry about it. I remember a buddy of mine, a guy named Preston Peterson, got to play with the Dallas Cowboys. He told me about how in one of his first games the ball was kicked away from him, so he was standing there watching. This big lineman came up and just knocked the hell out of him, and said, 'Welcome to the NFL.' I sort of adopted that because when you're born in America, you face the attitude of white supremacy. That's the field. You know you're going to get hit, so don't even worry about it. Just get up, go into the game, put on your shoulder pads, go get your college degree, and work, knowing that you're going to get hit. If you sit up and say, 'Oh, this white person might do this to us, might do that to us,' you might as well stay in bed. You never will step on that field. It's like when it rains: Do you wake up in the morning and say, 'It's raining, I can't go to work, I'm going to get wet'? If so, you lost already. Now, a lot of us wake up like that, but once you say that, once your mind is already committed to thinking that you can't go there, you can't do it."

One thing I asked a lot of people in these interviews is whether they think blacks today understand all the sacrifices older people made to put us in a situation to be successful. Acknowledging those who've done what I call the heavy lifting. I don't care whether it's competing in sports or acting or education or medicine, there has to be an acknowledgment of what came before you and how difficult that was.

"I don't think they wake up in the morning and say, 'I'm motivated to do better because Martin Luther King died, black people stood in front of dogs and fire hoses, and people were killed in Mississippi during the civil rights freedom marches,'" Bob said. "They don't think of it like that. They think of it almost in a way where they say, 'We're going to go out and get ours; I'm going to get it done.' They think of it in more individual ways; they don't think of it as collective. Although sometimes people say to me that they admire me or appreciate what I do, as a group I don't think young people today sit back and say, 'I owe what I have to those who went before me.'

"They know it, but I don't think it's the main driver for them. The main driver for them is to get out there and do their own thing but not as some recognition of what went before them. I hear what you're saying in terms of the fact that everybody stands on somebody else's shoulders. It's a nice thing to think, but I don't think they use it as their model or their guide as to what they do. They think, 'I'm entitled, just as anybody else is, to do this and get that.' All the young people I come in contact with believe in themselves, they work hard, they want to do it. They may respect what's gone before them, they understand it, they recognize it, but that's not what motivates them. I think what motivates them is the desire to better themselves, to do what their parents want them to do. But it's not seen as the social movement that it was before."

I came along at a time when we had obvious leaders in black communities, men like Dr. King, Malcolm X, Medgar Evers, and Muhammad Ali when it came to certain things. Is it reasonable to expect that we'll ever have leaders like that again?

"I don't think we have those kinds of leaders anymore, who sort of galvanize everybody," Bob said, "but I think we have them in sectors. In order to have a great leader you've got to have a great cause, and I don't think we have today the same great causes that we had when Martin Luther King could clearly be a leader. Or even Marcus Garvey or Booker T. Washington, because if you think about it, right now you've got forty percent of black folks who would say they're middle class, you've got another forty percent who would say they're underclass, and another ten or twenty percent who might say they're upper class. What are they all pushing toward? Some people say, you have to fight for better education. Well, some people who make money get an opportunity, and what do they do? Move their kids out of the neighborhood, go to the suburban schools. Others say there have got to be more jobs, more work. It's not where we're all reading off the same script, and if you're not reading off the same script, it's hard to have people rally behind one leader.

"Mr. Farrakhan has a different approach to galvanizing black folks. The Million Man March was an example. But it didn't really penetrate a lot of the other religious groups and the church leaders. Jesse Jackson and Al Sharpton play at the political level, but they couldn't come together on a common agenda. I think unless there is another movement of black folks, you're going to continue to have drifting and splintered leadership. Right now, Oprah is a leader for a whole lot of folks. Michael Jordan's a leader for a whole lot of folks. But if you were to say, 'Okay, somebody issue a call. We've got to have a meeting, it's critical, we've got to have everybody there.' I don't know anybody who could make that call and get everybody in the room.

"There's no clarion call. There's nothing that says, okay, let's rally around this cause. Without that, I'm afraid that we just drift into our own enclave. You go to your house, I go to my house; you go to this golf club, I go to that golf club; you vacation here, I vacation there. And what brings us together? That's the only thing that I think is missing with black folks: something that brings us together that we're all concerned about. It's not politics, because that's not the driver anymore. It's not religion as such. It's not a particular movement like Black Power. Right now, I guarantee you that there's nobody who can push a Rolodex button, and say—pick a number, the top 200, the top 150 black folks—we're going to meet to talk about this. Nobody can do it, nobody."

While Bill Cosby's statements weren't really the kind of clarion call Bob was talking about, I wondered what he thought about them, the challenge Cosby put forth for blacks to stop blaming whites and look inward at what can be done about teen pregnancy, about black-on-black crime, and the criticisms he made that became a huge controversy.

"I think Cosby said the right stuff; he's saying what a lot of people feel," Bob said. "I think what happened, though, is that it came out the wrong way. To say young people have to be able to speak English to go to work or school, and you can't go around using drugs and committing crimes—I think everybody agrees with that. But when he delivered the message, it was almost like he was saying, 'You people. It's not me, it's not my family, it's not my kids, it's you people.'

"Some people responded, 'Okay, Bill, show me what you've done besides be on television and done good stuff on the shows. Show me, you know, where you've been down in the trenches with them. Show me where you've been out on the front lines.' Bill could have said, 'Look, I'm going to come down there and I'm going to work in the classroom.' I mean, it kind of came across as if he was talking down to people. He's got a great reputation as a great personality, great comedian, great philanthropist, but I don't know anybody who would say, 'I've seen him in Cabrini Green. He's been over in the ghetto in a real meaningful way.' So some people felt, 'Who are you? When's the last time you woke up with a family of eight kids and the mother's twenty-eight and your daddy ain't around? Why you telling me what I should do?' So that's what I think the problem was with Bill's statements. It seemed like they were coming from somebody who was just a little bit removed from the issue. It can be dangerous for somebody to say, 'I made it; now you got a responsibility to make it like I did,' as opposed to saying, 'What can I do to help you? How can I help you to make it like me? I'm going out and I'm going to issue a call to Bob Johnson, to Charles Barkley, let's all come together and have a discussion and figure out what we're going to do.' That, I think, would have been a far better approach. But what he said was what a lot of people are saying. I tell my kids that you can't walk into a room and expect to get a job if you can't communicate."

Consider all that Bob has accomplished. Long before he started BET and made his name, he created wealth and understood business in a way that ought to inspire people, whether or not they watch or appreciate his network. You don't often see Johnson quoted on how he would counsel black kids growing up on how to be successful.

"Well, first of all, you cannot let the belief that white people are superior to you stop you from doing what you want to do, which translates into you have to believe in yourself," he said. "If you believe in yourself, that's number one. Second is you've got to be willing to work hard. Nobody gives you anything; it doesn't happen overnight. You have to be willing to stay in the trenches and work hard. And third is you've got to understand how to communicate effectively across all different levels of interaction. You have to learn how to interpret people and understand what they want from you and what you can give to them. And that goes into believing in yourself. I don't care if you're going to sweep the streets; be the best street sweeper you can be. If you go in there with that attitude, that I'm as good as the next guy, you may not end up being the richest guy in the world, you may not end up being the best ballplayer in the world, you may not end up being a senator from Illinois. But you're going to know in your mind that you are doing the best you can do based on your belief in yourself.

"That's one thing that I've had to have all along. When I got started, I'm in a room with nothing but white folks at Princeton University, I'm in a room with nothing but white folks in the cable industry, and I'm saying to myself, 'These guys ain't rocket scientists. They ain't the smartest people in the world. They don't just go around and all of a sudden money falls in. They happen to be whites who believe in themselves because they've got a belief that they're from a superior group of people.' I know when you walked on the court, you knew by the end of the night, on average, you'd have eighteen points, thirteen rebounds, seven blocked shots. The other guy might walk in saying, 'Man, I don't know if I can get any; maybe I can get two or three.'

"We have to say to our young people, 'Believe in yourself. Don't look across at some white person and say, I think skin color already gives them fifteen points. If you believe that your success level is defined by what your color is or where your parents came from or where you came from, the game is lost. The game is lost.' I grew up in a family with ten kids. First one in my family who went to college. My folks were day workers all their lives. I'd walk into classrooms for the first time and I would think all the white people knew each other. I mean, they'd all sit around mingling and you'd think they all knew each other. The first time I flew on a plane, Charles, I'm like twenty. And I'm sitting next to white boys . . . maybe twelve and nine, looked like they were reading *The Wall Street Journal,* discussing what colleges they're going to go to. And I'm thinking, 'They are so ahead of us.' Then as I got a little bit older, I started listening to them. I'm in the cable business with Ted Turner, and I said, 'Wait a minute, he's got access to a little bit more money than I do, but other than that, that's it.'

"If we had the confidence in ourselves that we were just as good, we would overcome this other thing that we have: this sort of self-hatred. I think today eighty percent of our problem is in ourselves and twenty percent is in systemic racism. If you look at the NBA and the fact that the owners own the teams and the players play, well, that ain't got nothing to do with the owners being smarter than the players. All that's got to do with is the fact that when the money was accumulated first, black folks were denied access to wealth-creation opportunities. We were denied education. We were denied the opportunity to get federal government grants, federal government TV licenses, government grants for oil and mineral rights. We weren't given all that. Rockefeller made his money off government granted rights. The guys who built the railroads—the government granted them the rights-of-way. We show up and say, 'We want a radio frequency.' Well, first of all, they say, 'You've got to be educated.' Okay, okay. Second of all, 'You've got to prove that you can operate a radio station—have you ever operated one before?' No, I haven't operated one before. 'And, by the way, you've got to have money to operate it.' You go to a bank, and they ask, 'Well, have you operated one before? No? We can't loan you money.' It's no wonder that all the banks and all the mineral rights are owned by white people, and most of the radio stations are government frequencies.

"There's only one reason I'm in the NBA today. It's not because they wanted black folks. It's because they wanted $300 million and I happened to have it. If I didn't have $300 million, there wouldn't be a black owner. No one said, 'Look, we really want Bob in this league, he's a really good guy, but he can only pay $200 million, so let's give him a $100-million discount. Then all of us good folks who recognize affirmative action, instead of getting that $10 million apiece that we were going to get from him if he'd paid $300 million, let's only get $7 million apiece.' Hell, no!

"What happens is this: If you start off a game, one guy has all the poker chips over here, and you just got a few of them. He's always going to beat you 'cause he can take more risks than you can take. You can afford to lose one or two, but he can lose ten and still be ahead of you. What happens in this society is we wake up and think, 'All the poker chips are over there and now we got to try to get them.' Then it becomes a mental thing: 'They're better than us and that's why they got all the poker chips.' The people we should be helping do it— our own people—we don't trust, and, by the way, once we get it, some-times we forget the people there keep thinking, 'Divide and conquer,' and they can buy us off. All of a sudden Motown is doing good and making money, and it's all a black business. Along came Columbia and said, 'Gee you know what? Barry's paying you $15 million for the next five albums; I'll give you $30 million.' Now that's the way the sys-tem is. That's the way it is. But you can't blame anybody for doing that.

"When I sold BET to Viacom, some folks said, why didn't you sell BET to a black company? Logical question. But that would have meant somebody black would have had to have $3 billion, and not only $3 billion in stocks, because I had to buy and sell it to them in cash or I would have had to pay taxes on it. So it created a hurdle that was impossible. That hurdle started a long time ago and the only way we overcome that is believing in ourselves and working with each other and insisting that we get our fair share. Yeah, you vote early and often, you fight injustice every time you see it, but if we don't compete and we mentally think they have a better chance of winning, the game's over. I can tell you in a minute that anytime you walk into a room and you're thinking that white folks are better, the game's over. The other thing is that they don't think about us as much as we think of them. See, we sit back thinking that white people think of us all the time. No. They think of themselves. The only time that we pop up is when something happens that causes them to focus on us. The other thing is that once they build a relationship with one of us, that satisfies their need to be sort of liberal or diverse, and that's it, they got enough. Still, the bottom line is that if you sit back and worry about it, you'll never get there."

The issue, of course, is whether Bob Johnson sees that kind of toughness, that sense of competition. Confidence is a great thing, but you have to have a reason to be confident. You have to have developed the set of skills to go out and compete. I don't care how confident a guy is that he is going to beat me; if he doesn't have the skills necessary, the confidence isn't going to do him any good. I worry about that, and I wonder if when Bob looks and interacts with young black people whether he is worried, as well.

"Worried is probably too strong," he said. "I feel concerned because there doesn't seem to be a philosophy out there. There doesn't seem to be an ideology of what we're about. At the same time when I talk to young people, they seem to want to be around black folks who are doing positive things. They want to be exposed to people like you or me who are doing things because they want some comfort to know that they're accepted by somebody.

"During the civil rights movement people came together for a common cause. They felt camaraderie in doing it together. Right now, if it's just compete for money, once you get the house, the car, the boat, the bling-bling or whatever, then you can say, 'Well, who do I trust? Who do I want to go on vacation with? Who do I want to hang with? Who can I sit down and drink with and let my hair down and just relax and not always feel like I've got to be up on point and everything else?' That's what they don't really have and I think that's the only thing that concerns me. I think it's our responsibility to try to generate that. When you sit down and talk with some of the guys who play ball or some of the hip-hop guys like P. Diddy and Jay-Z, they tell you, 'Man, look, what can we do together? I want to be involved in stuff you're involved in. I want to know what you're doing.' That's what I hear from them anyway."

Obviously, the young people Bob Johnson is hanging with tend to be rich guys, like him. Do kids in middle-class or poor families feel the same way? I tend to think they do, even if they won't say so. And I liked what he said about kids looking for companionship and even leadership from their elders. It just might mean they're open to the good lessons lots of folks have to teach. I like that a lot.

KICKING IT AROUND

A CONVERSATION WITH MORGAN FREEMAN

It's so great to be able to watch Morgan Freeman act, whether he's playing a president or a pimp. He's been one of America's greatest actors for years and years. But he never got a leading role in a movie until he was fifty years old, which is really sad for moviegoers given how talented the man is, how accomplished he was in the theater, and how much better off the movie industry would have been by calling him to Hollywood earlier.

He earned Oscar nominations for *Driving Miss Daisy, Glory, The Shawshank Redemption,* and *Million Dollar Baby.* He was never cast as a romantic lead or had so much as a female love interest in a movie, yet he keeps distinguishing himself and the movies he's in, from *Street Smart* with the late Christopher Reeve and Mimi Rogers to *Unforgiven* with Clint Eastwood and Gene Hackman to *Sum of All Fears* with Ben Affleck.

When Mr. Freeman agreed to talk to me and Mike Wilbon over dinner one night in Manhattan, I wasn't sure where to start. I wanted his views on his career, of course, and the movie industry and the industry as it relates to black folks. But I also wanted to just listen to him on any number of topics and issues. An actor isn't all Morgan Freeman is. We just knew the conversation would be fascinating, and it was, so we jumped right into it. It was fascinating to listen to a man who has every reason to be bitter but isn't, a man who has no interest in accepting the status quo or looking for the easy answer.

BARKLEY: One thing that's been interesting in these interviews is that all the people we've talked to say we're not so stupid as to think that racism does not exist, but now the divide is more because of economics.

FREEMAN: It is. We are way more class-separated now than we are by race.

WILBON: Is that a step in the right direction?

FREEMAN: Listen, why worry about it? Why struggle if you don't want to improve your standing, you know? Drive your BMW and live in your four-bedroom house. It's not a serious wrong at all. Look at you, Charles. You're sitting here looking back at the little town that you grew up in and you're talking from this lofty perspective that you have now. How difficult was it for you?

BARKLEY: Very . . . I'll accept some credit. . . . But why did I get all this, while that guy who keeps bringing our drinks for us, he's working his butt off, too?

FREEMAN: You want me to say that's the breaks? What else can we do? We can ask what your obligation is if you have a talent. Maybe when this guy goes home, he goes right to his computer, and he's busy writing something that, who knows, five years from now will be the—

BARKLEY: Greatest thing in the world. I know, but the way I look at my life is, like, not that I'm a religious fanatic, but I ask myself why did the Lord give me this great opportunity to be in this position to play basketball for sixteen years, now to be on TV every week? You know, I just feel like I'm blessed and lucky.

FREEMAN: Well, Charles, Denzel Washington has a saying that I really like: "You say the good Lord gave you this; I say the good Lord probably just gave you the talent." You had to develop it on your own. And then you had to keep tap dancing in order to make it work for you. If you have talent without that tap dance, you're just another dude with some talent that nobody knows about. There's millions of those. I'm not quite sure that the Lord wants all the credit you're giving him. One thing that's really clear that I like in *Bruce Almighty* is that the most important thing God gave you was free will. Then it's up to you what to do with it.

BARKLEY: You know, I was excited to meet you tonight. It's really an honor and pleasure to meet you.

FREEMAN: Really?

BARKLEY: Yeah, I'm a movie guy. I love movies. So I just want to thank you for everything you've done. But I'm also wondering: Are you happy, sad, disappointed, frustrated at all the doors you have opened? Do you think black actors that have come after you have taken it to the next level? 'Cause when I played basketball, I felt like all the older black guys before me, I had an obligation to them to do good, not to screw it up.

FREEMAN: I think that life moves forward, it moves on. I don't want anybody to feel obligated to me for what I've done. I didn't do anything for anybody else; I did it for my own sake. But I know who was ahead of me and what they did and how they did it. I'm talking Sidney Poitier, Sammy Davis Jr., all the guys who are able to get past a certain barrier and keep on stepping. So that's my only obligation. I think that's all anybody else's obligation. I pay deep homage to Sidney.

BARKLEY: But I think all blacks who succeed in a specialized field have to pay homage to the past, because I look at guys like Dr. J, Bill Russell, those guys, I owed them, because they did what I considered the heavy lifting. No matter what racism we might experience today, I don't think we can compare it to what blacks felt in their day. I truly believe that in my heart. What obligation do younger blacks have to those who opened doors? . . . I guess that's what I'm asking.

FREEMAN: None. Your obligation is to yourself. If you have a talent for anything, your obligation is to that. Make that work the best you can, and I think everything just falls in its own place. I don't know that you have to live your life outside the boundaries of your own needs. That's all I'm doing. If someone calls me and says, "We're doing such and such for Sidney Poitier . . . whomever," I'll be there, to stand and say thank you. But it's not like I'm going to wake up in the morning and go and live my life in an exemplary way because of Sidney. I don't know that I owe anybody anything except myself.

BARKLEY: See, that's where we just disagree. Every time I played basketball, I felt a great obligation. I realized I was going to make a lot more money than those guys, I was going to have a high profile. But they opened all the doors and put me in that situation. I think if I were blessed to be put in that situation, I always thought it was important that I didn't screw it up.

FREEMAN: I know I didn't rise up on my own. But I'm saying I don't think there is an obligation.

BARKLEY: Did you see that story in the paper about graduation rates for athletes? You see basketball went down again. I have a problem with that 'cause the majority of the basketball players are black. It's decreased for something like the fifth straight season. And football has risen, but it's only up to like right around fifty percent. But basketball went down to like thirty percent now. That ain't right, man. Colleges have an obligation to educate those kids. They have an obligation. When they're making tens of millions of dollars on those kids, they have an obligation. I'm sensitive, because I'm black, and the majority of those college kids who play college basketball are black. For the fifth year in a row, their graduation rate has gone down? That ain't right.

FREEMAN: But don't take all the responsibility away from the kids.

BARKLEY: They are kids.

FREEMAN: They're kids, but that does not take away their own choice-making ability. They've got parents also.

BARKLEY: See this is where we disagree, respectfully disagree. When I was eighteen, I wasn't a good student, and my college coach came to me, and said, "Charles, you want to play basketball or you want to get your degree?" I said I want to play basketball. I don't think that's a fair question for a man in power to ask an eighteen-year-old with no wherewithal to answer. None. I'm not going to say I want to get my degree. I'm going to say I want to play basketball. I'd rather they say, "If you don't go to class and get your degree, you're not going to play basketball." It's really up to the individual coach. Dean Smith made sure his players graduated. . . . Where were you born?

FREEMAN: I was born in Memphis, but that was just a fluke.

BARKLEY: When did you move to Mississippi? How did you get there?

FREEMAN: Well, I grew up there, and then I got out of there and I traveled a lot. But even with all the problems we have down there, I was never as comfortable anywhere else as I am there. We're an agrarian society, lots of unemployment, so we're basically poor. I'm well off, so I say go somewhere you'll be useful. I started going back to visit my parents back in the seventies. Then, the older they got, the more I went home, and the more I went home, the more I realized—

BARKLEY: They needed you?

FREEMAN: It wasn't that they needed me. I needed them. . . . I needed to be there. When we get home, my wife wakes up at the crack of dawn and she's out in the fields, she's out digging up things, planting trees. It was definitely going home: safety, comfort, ease. I have such a wonderful place there; it's like an oasis.

BARKLEY: Do you get involved in politics in Mississippi?

FREEMAN: The only time I really got political was when we were trying to get rid of the Confederate flag in Mississippi. We still got it. You know what I'm going to do? I'm going to join the Klan. You can't beat 'em, join 'em.

BARKLEY: The governor of Mississippi, Haley Barbour, the first thing he did was put the Confederate flag back on the police cars in Mississippi when he got elected this year. I have zero respect for anybody with a Confederate flag, zero.

FREEMAN: Zero. It represents three things to me: intolerance, treason, and stupidity.

BARKLEY: There is a thing in America called common courtesy. Just out of common courtesy for my fellow human being, if there's something that offends them, I'm not going to have it. But not everybody's like that. And it amazes me how many people still put up the Confederate flag when it offends so many people. Like with NASCAR . . .

FREEMAN: Say nothing bad about NASCAR, Charles.

BARKLEY: I've got a little hate for NASCAR.

FREEMAN: Don't say nothing bad about NASCAR.

WILBON: You a NASCAR fan?

FREEMAN: Big time.

BARKLEY: Two of my friends are Jeff Gordon and Kevin Harvick. You know I'm a sports junkie; I almost cried the day Dale Earnhardt Sr. died. But I tried to go to two races. The first one, I never got there. There were Confederate flags all over. And it wasn't like, oh, a couple. It seemed like thirty thousand Confederate flags, on their trailers and everywhere. That means to me: Do Not Enter. And they're like, oh, that's just an Alabama thing. I said, well, I'll go to Atlanta. So I go to a race in Atlanta, and it was the same thing. I said, "I can't go to this."

FREEMAN: I've never been. I can't go to these places, 'cause I can't do crowds. I mean, I've driven, I had lessons, and—

BARKLEY: The drivers are nice guys. They've got the best endorsement deals out of all of the jocks, too. That's what we need.

WILBON: Only one NBA player got something from his jersey.

FREEMAN: Jordan.

BARKLEY: For the last thirty years, NBA players haven't gotten anything, but in the last year, we get $25 million out of $2 billion to put them on the players. In NASCAR, any money you make with your picture, shirt, sweater, whatever—you get it. They got the best deal. They're unbelievable. Dale Earnhardt Sr. was probably the richest athlete in the world because they split whatever they make on coffee mugs, bumper stickers, tons of stuff. They don't have that big of a fan base, but they sell that stuff and they get the money. Now, I want to ask you another question, but I don't want you to think that I'm slighting you in any way. Have you ever been frustrated that a guy who's not as great as you are has gotten more money because he was white?

FREEMAN: No.

BARKLEY: Never?

FREEMAN: No.

BARKLEY: Do you think that's a fair question?

FREEMAN: Yeah. The most frustrating time I had was when Cleavon Little, another black actor, used to get all the breaks.

BARKLEY: Let's take Jim Carrey, who is white and also a good actor. He's younger and he's probably always going to make more money than you. That's never had you frustrated?

FREEMAN: No . . . because after you make enough money that you can't spend it, everything else is just numbers. I tell my agent every now and then, "You know, we make a lot of money. Let's just find us something good to do."

WILBON: That's similar to what Sam Jackson told us. He said he told his agent, in essence, I don't want to audition for that role. I want to play something different every time. I'm not playing that character again. To me, that would seem very freeing: the ability to choose what you want to do. Not being presumptuous, but Sidney Poitier did not have that freedom.

FREEMAN: No, he did not. He could choose what he wanted to do, but he couldn't choose what he did not want to do.

BARKLEY: Who is the black actor, in your generation, who's never gotten the credit or respect he deserves?

FREEMAN: In my generation? Nobody.

BARKLEY: Nobody?

FREEMAN: No, all the ones that deserve it got it as far as I know. [silence for about five seconds] I mean, can you think of someone? You got a name in mind?

BARKLEY: What about Ossie Davis?

FREEMAN: Well, he's a generation ahead of me, but I think for what Ossie did and what he wanted, he was in some really terrific movies. He was in *The Hill* with Sean Connery. He was in *The Scalp Hunters* with Burt Lancaster. And he wrote *Purlie Victorious*. I don't think he's been slighted at all. You know, all of us are up and down; nobody's writing about you every day. You happen to have a show and that's great, but the time will come when somebody will say, "Whatever happened to Morgan Freeman?"

WILBON: I hope you're a long ways from that.

FREEMAN: Me, too, but that time's coming. And I don't want anybody to say, "Well, I don't think he ever got the respect that he deserves." I think you get what you deserve. There are some people who are on the wrong end of the log. And they will live the rest of their lives not moving. I think I would beat the log along and walk someplace else. And people say, "Well, I could have done this or that, but I have other obligations." That is the choice you make. But all your life is about choice.

WILBON: I think part of what Charles is talking about is that—right or wrong—success is so much defined in our culture by financial wealth and acclaim. Not that it should be, but that is often the measuring stick.

FREEMAN: I can't deny what you're saying is true. But you will measure your own success. People say to me, "When do you feel you were successful?" I was successful, absolutely, when I got my first job in New York City on the stage. Didn't have to wait tables, drive a cab, or shine shoes. I think that's why I have mixed feelings about affirmative action. There is part of me that understands very clearly that the playing field is not level, and something should be done about that institutionally. Just as race was set up as a barrier, it should be set up as a way to level the playing field. I feel that in all but one part of me. The other part of me says, "Don't give me anything. Just don't make it stand in my way."

BARKLEY: Now, let me ask you this question. Sometimes I don't feel comfortable with the way black people are portrayed on television and in film.

FREEMAN: Look, a lot of people had problems with that movie *Soul Plane.* But we got to allow ourselves to do what we want to do, too, you know? I mean these guys doing the lampoons like that, they make a lot of money. Everything doesn't have to be holy. We can't hold everybody to your standard or my standard with this, you know? I've been invited to be involved in movies like that.

WILBON: To which you said . . .

FREEMAN: I said, it's not my cup of tea, I appreciate your thinking about me, but it's not my thing.

BARKLEY: That's a conscious effort you made, though, right?

FREEMAN: No, at no time in my life can I remember ever wanting to be or leaning in the direction of comedy.

WILBON: Sam [Jackson] told us the most important word in Hollywood is "no." It's no.

FREEMAN: Let me tell you, it really is the most powerful word. You tell somebody no, they look around; you've got their attention. Now you know how much flak Sam has gotten in his career because he has no compunction about using the word *nigger.*

WILBON: Right. He gets into that role and that character.

FREEMAN: Yeah, yeah. "What is *your* problem?" That's his feeling, you know? But I just thought, "Sam, you shouldn't have done that."

BARKLEY: Is the N word a generational thing?

FREEMAN: Somebody said one time we only have one sure designation, one that's going to stay with us forever. It started out with colored, then it became Negro, then you got Afro-American, then you got to black, and now we're at African American. The N word transcends all that. It hasn't gone away and it still serves a purpose. Generationally, I don't know. It depends on us, y'all.

WILBON: Even though so many actors and actresses of color are accomplished, it seems to take so long, there's so much work, there's so much achievement before a break comes to be in a feature film, a film that's going to have mass distribution. With your New York stage work and all the things you had done before, did you wonder if the - break—

FREEMAN: Would ever come?

WILBON: Or it didn't matter to you because you loved the work so much?

FREEMAN: No, my whole life early on was about movies. I really wanted to be in a movie. The first job I got was on the stage in 1967. Then, if you were working in New York, people would come to see you and say, "Oh, man, this is going to take you to the coast. This is it." Then, it wouldn't happen. A lot of people left here in the seventies for the West Coast, and I was still here. And I had thought, maybe I'll just give that up and settle down here, just do this, you know? Then, you know, it happens. Before that, I had called my agent up one day and said, "I think I'm going to go out to California, man, because that's where everybody's going and everybody's working." He said, "Yeah, but how many times do you see them in the movies? If I were you, I wouldn't go. When Hollywood wants you, they'll send for you." Took about five years, and they sent for me.

WILBON: What was the movie?

FREEMAN: It wasn't a movie at all; it was a TV show, "Farmstown USA." In 1983, 1984, somewhere in there. I may be wrong about that.

BARKLEY: So when you played the president of the United States, did you ever say, damn, I made it, I really made it? I know I've had a great, great, great career. But when a black man gets to play the president, it's kind of like . . . wow. That's when you know everybody knows you're great at what you do.

FREEMAN: I never thought about it like that. I should have, I suppose. I just thought that now they want me to play the president, and I'll do it.

WILBON: Just another role?

FREEMAN: Yeah, another role. I remember somebody in Denver said to me, "Well, you got to play a black president." And I said, "No. No. I've never played a black anything. I did not play a black president. I can't play black. I am black."

BARKLEY: It's very interesting to me that when some movie comes out, why do they describe it as a black movie? They don't describe other movies as white movies. We interviewed George Lopez talking about how they'll say about his show, "Oh, it's a Latino show."

FREEMAN: I think it's like a point of boasting there. You won't see them in any other countries, who say, well look at what our colored guys can do.

BARKLEY: It makes it harder for the black or Hispanic guys to succeed when they do that.

FREEMAN: They're not trying to make it harder; they really are not. The one thing I've come to appreciate about this business: It is about money.

BARKLEY: That's what Peter Guber said when he was talking about why he did *The Color Purple.* He was saying, yeah I wanted to act like I did the project out of a sense of social contribution, but the fact is, doing this movie with black actors and targeting black audiences is good business. It surprised me that he was that honest. He said we were missing a whole audience out there.

FREEMAN: Well, that was why that blaxploitation period of movies got going. You know, *Shaft* and everything. The first one was *Cotton Comes to Harlem;* that movie made so much money.

BARKLEY: Is there one part that you want to play that you haven't found a script for yet?

FREEMAN: Yeah, there is. Back in 1875, when the American government decided that manifest destiny went beyond the Mississippi River, they decided, well, we're going to have to push on. Everything from Portsmouth, Arkansas, west was the badlands, Indian territory, and everybody who wanted to get away from the law was over there. Just mostly in north Texas, Oklahoma, and those environs. The government really wanted to open Oklahoma up for land, not taking account of the Indians. So they sent a federal judge named Issac Parker to Portsmouth and across the Arkansas River into Indian territory. He hired about 220, 250 deputy marshals, black, white, and red, and their job was to go get the miscreants and bring them to justice. One of the baddest among these marshals was a guy named Bad Bass Reeds. Bass served as a cop from 1875, and he died in 1927 in Muskogee. He'd just retired from the police force about four years before that. He was a bad ass. I want to play him.

BARKLEY: Have you ever directed anything?

FREEMAN: Yeah, I directed a movie called *Bopha!* with Danny Glover and Alfre Woodard. It was a South African story.

WILBON: Is that a passion, or just something you dabbled in?

FREEMAN: No, just something. I wanted to find out if I had any talent for it. And I did. But I found out I've been spoiled by acting. I can do four movies and make four times as much money off of each movie as I can directing one.

WILBON: How hard will it be to get the Bass project done?

FREEMAN: I'm pushing harder right now. I've been working on Bass for over twelve years now. It's just hard to get a script. I know what I want, the studios want one thing, other people want another . . .

BARKLEY: Studios want something that's going to make money.

FREEMAN: But you don't know what's going to make money. That's the thing. You don't know what's going to make money.

BARKLEY: What's more important . . . ? This is a loaded question, actually.

FREEMAN: Okay, I'll be careful.

BARKLEY: What's more important to you: critical acclaim or box office?

FREEMAN: Without box office, you don't get no critical acclaim, 'cause you can't make it.

BARKLEY: Have you ever done a part you thought was great that didn't do well at the box office?

FREEMAN: Yeah. *The Shawshank Redemption* died at the box office. It did okay overseas, but it didn't do really well until they started selling it as a DVD. The problem is, it's a great movie, but you have to be able to say the title. I go to you, and I say, "Man, I saw this fabulous movie. It's called the ahh, ahhh, ahh. Shenshampt or something." You're dead, you know? That was the problem with *Shawshank Redemption*. The title of the book was *Rita Hayworth and the Shawshank Redemption*. I said, "Well, why didn't you use the real title?" Well, it wouldn't fit on the marquis. I said, "Well, use 'Rita Hayworth.' " That fit on the marquis. You could just put "Rita Hayworth." They could have called it anything but *The Shawshank Redemption*.

WILBON: What did you like when you went to the movies when you were growing up? I've heard my father's stories about Georgia, where they could sit and what theaters they could go to. What was it like for you in Mississippi?

FREEMAN: We went to the Paramount, and we'd sit in the balcony. Yeah, that was in the forties and fifties.

WILBON: What grabbed you about the movies?

FREEMAN: Everything, everything. I went to the movies the first time when I was about six and a half years old. In Charleston, we didn't even have a movie theater, and still don't. But when I went to Chicago, my parents would take me to the movies. Man, I was just enthralled. Then I got onstage and felt this is where I belong. All my teachers, everybody said, boy, we know where you're going. So I always knew.

America is great that way. Morgan Freeman knew growing up that he was going to be an actor, and here he is. And I always loved basketball. But not everyone who wants to be an actor or a professional athlete can make it. And most kids don't have their path marked for them that way. So what about them? What about everyone else? There's no subject more important to this discussion than education, which is why I was glad my final conversation was with Marian Wright Edelman.

ON OUR WATCH

MARIAN WRIGHT EDELMAN

If you want to know what life is like today for many children, especially disadvantaged black children, there's no one better to talk to than Marian Wright Edelman. She's been on the front lines fighting for children her entire career. Beginning in the sixties, she was the first black woman admitted to the Mississippi bar, and she directed the NAACP's Legal Defense and Educational Fund in Jackson, Mississippi. Since then, her efforts have joined together advocacy with information-gathering and training—all directed toward solving the problems of disadvantaged Americans. In 1973, she created the Children's Defense Fund, a private nonprofit foundation with the mission of providing a strong, effective voice for all the children of America who cannot vote, lobby, or speak for themselves.

For forty years, Marian has been a strong force for all the things children need in life: family support, education, medical care, and a sense of self-worth. For those efforts she's been honored with such awards as the Albert Schweitzer Prize for Humanitarianism, a MacArthur Foundation prize fellowship, the Robert F. Kennedy Lifetime Achievement Award, and the Presidential Medal of Freedom.

This woman is a hero—and a leader. I'd put her right up there with some of my other heroes. Magic Johnson, for instance, has become a real role model of mine with what he's doing in inner cities around the country. He understands what having fame means. You're not famous just to make money and have a big house and a big car. Oprah's fantastic, too. She had me on her show and she's been amazing to me. She does so much good with her show, plus she has all kinds of charitable activities. And I really love Joe Brown. I never met him, but I watch his show a lot. He's strong on just being a man and doing the right thing.

So I asked Marian, do we have great black leaders but not enough people know about them? Or, do we not have the right kind of black leaders today? Why don't our young people listen to them?

"Well, there are a lot of different questions," said Marian. "And there are wonderful black leaders in communities all across the country, but they haven't, of course, been elevated up to the national level in the same way as when you had a Dr. King in that old era. I think we're at the most dangerous time ever—we're really going backwards, and at times like this, I think having positive images about black folks and about the progress we've made is especially necessary. At the Children's Defense Fund, we've tried to do something about the fact that everybody's images of young black folks are of the ones who are killing somebody or on drugs. About twelve years ago, with the help of black entertainment executives, including Bob Johnson, we began to celebrate kids who are beating the odds. There are a bunch of them out there and they're the most inspiring folks ever. Lifting up and celebrating success and strength is absolutely crucial. Some of the young people are listening if we provide them another voice and provide them opportunities to serve and to be useful.

"We adults have dropped the ball. One of the most important questions we face is, how do we build a successful generation of young leaders committed to service and to their community? We're running Freedom Schools every summer for about five thousand disadvantaged kids. About a third to a half of the instructors are black males who come out of inner cities who are teaching kids from inner cities that there's another way. I'm very moved by them. They are spiritually hungry. They are becoming competent. It's about making reading and academic performance exciting, but it also is about serving. We have ninety-five percent parent involvement. If you grab these kids, give 'em something that's an alternative to the messages of the street, I'll tell you: They'll take it. We have one young man, Rodney Johnson, whose mother was in prison and who had been treated violently. He went off to Spelman College and is now a resident at Harvard Medical School, after finishing his medical training there.

"But for every one of those who is beating the odds, there are nine who are not. So one of the things that must be part of this conversation is talking honestly about the problems and talking honestly and strongly about the need for personal responsibility and the role of parents and adult role models. We've got a lot of grandmammas who ought to be given Nobel Peace prizes. We're struggling to raise children without adequate support. We've also got to look at the structural and systemic changes that make it very hard for families to form. Benjamin Franklin said a long time ago that the best family formation policy is a good job. People who don't have jobs can't marry and support a family. A lot of folks are trying to do the right thing by their children, but they can't find a job, and even when they're working, they can't earn above the minimum wage. I can take you to see them. We've got to talk about children in the context of families, in the context of community, and in the context of national choices.

"We've certainly seen enormous progress since *Brown v. Board of Education*. Look at where you are and the representation we have in sports and many other areas. We have the largest number of elected black officials in Mississippi of any state. Look at where Colin Powell is—it's enormous progress. But there's been another story that's been happening over the last twenty years that we're going to have to dissect. Large parts of our black population have been going backwards. Black males have been particularly affected. I don't know that we fully understand all of it, but we have this dichotomy in black America: While the top has been rising, the bottom has been going backwards. I always like to say that the top can't stay up there without the bottom.

"We're going to issue a report, 'The Cradle to Prison Pipeline.' A black boy born in 2001 has a one in three chance of ending up in prison. That's a disaster. For the black family, there's nobody for young women to marry. The young men go into prison, and when they come out, they can't vote and they can't get a job. Zero tolerance policies in schools, zero tolerance policy in the courts, three strikes you're out, and drugs have really put us back on a path that's so scary. We've all got to raise the alarm."

With her dedication to helping young people, I wondered what Marian thought about what Bill Cosby said.

"Well, I agree with what Cosby said about the need for personal responsibility," she said. "In all of our films and all the things that we write, we talk about that. Don't have babies until you're ready to support them for a lifetime. Parents shouldn't have double standards. You tell your girls to stay chaste, you tell your boys to score. But we also need to talk about the culture. We adults send an absolutely hypocritical message. We tell teenaged kids in the inner city not to have babies, and then you put on the cover of *People* magazine all the Hollywood stars who've had babies out of wedlock. I mean, c'mon, let's get consistent here. And the hip-hop culture has many good strong features, but if you look at those videos, guns and glamour are a rite of passage.

"I'm just looking at the new child gun data that's come out this week; we lose more children every year to gun violence than ever before in American history. Each year. We've made progress. When we began the black community crusade for children in 1990, very quietly—in fact, that's where the original words 'Leave No Child Behind' came from, we trademarked that phrase—we did a poll of black children and black families, thinking they would talk to us about education, Head Start, health care, all things we thought we knew. We were stunned to hear that the greatest fear among black young people was that they wouldn't live to adulthood, that they were planning their own funerals. They felt totally hopeless. Black parents were worried that their children wouldn't live to adulthood. There was this pervasive hopelessness that just stunned me. Every year we issue an annual report: eighteen kids a day dying—more whites than blacks, but blacks disproportionately. Black children are dying ten minutes from the White House. And there is a kind of a hopelessness both in the inner cities and in my little hometown in Marlboro County, where there's nothing for them to do. The biggest business in town is the prison. We've got 580,000 black men in prison compared to about 45,000 who graduate from college each year.

"I say what Bill Cosby says, and many other people say it. We may say it in a different tone or different context, but we say it. However, what's missing is the other half: what's happened structurally in the economy, the impact of zero tolerance policies in schools, things like that. For our report on 'The Cradle to Prison Pipeline,' we had investigative reporters go out, and they found police are picking up six-year-olds for acting out in school. I understand the need for discipline in the classroom, but six-year-olds should not be picked up by police and put into jail and fingerprinted. Judges say they can't even see the faces of the kids above the table. The mental-health system is letting them down, the parents aren't able to meet their needs, and some of them are often battered. We know that parents need to be responsible, and grandparents need to be responsible, but I know an awful lot of mammas we deal with every day who are struggling. If you're working and you can't pay rent and you're in a homeless shelter, and you can't get child care and your Head Start is being cut and Early Head Start is reaching only three percent, and the choice of the nation is to give you a tax cut, something's wrong."

Since Marian agreed with Cosby on his basic message, I asked her why she thought he and others have been criticized inside the black community for taking a stance like that.

"It's because of how those comments are made; it's in the context," said Marian. "That night Cosby made his comments, we were celebrating the anniversary of *Brown,* and so the tone of his remarks seemed out of place. Even though I would say the same thing, I would say it in a different way. Saying those words at the moment without having the other fifty percent of the piece there leaves it incomplete, especially in a context where the external climate is terribly dangerous when the entire federal safety net and others are being dismantled. You can say the same thing, but you've got to also acknowledge progress and you've got to acknowledge that personal responsibility alone won't do it.

"You should talk to my nephew, who's the head of shock trauma at Johns Hopkins hospital. He patches up all these young kids who are coming in who are dying, coming in multiple times, and he's so concerned about the glamorization of violence. How do we have an alternative voice or neutralize the voices of the messages on MTV, so that we don't let kids think that it's cool to go out and have guns and shoot people? At the same time, more importantly, how do we have greater community responsibilities to counter it? The gangs and the drug dealers are open twenty-four hours a day, seven days a week. But the churches are closed, and the malls are closed. We don't have enough alternatives to the streets and enough of a positive vision. So I agree with the Cosby message, but it has to be put in a way that cannot be used just to say it's all about you not taking personal responsibility, when there aren't any jobs, Head Start and Early Head Start are being cut, health care is eroding, and the minimum wage leads to poverty. You've got to include both."

It seems pretty clear to me that part of the reason Cosby was criticized was that he made his comments in a public forum that was

aired on CNN. He was speaking to a predominantly black audience and he was talking about the black community, but it was going out to the world at large. People seem to have thought: Why are you airing our problems to the world when this is something we can handle within? There's just one problem: We aren't. And I'm pretty sure he wanted to get it out there.

The question is: When is the right time? If you do it privately, you're not going to affect that many people; whereas if you do it nationally, you start a conversation, so now we have everybody talking about it. We all can argue about whether it was the right place or the right time, but we all seem to agree that what he said was right. But both Edelman and Cosby are a little older than me, and I wondered if she'd gotten frustrated that all the hard work she had done in her day was now being undermined.

"You know, we have made a lot of progress," Marian said, "but, boy, you know, now Mr. Bush is trying to destroy it. We've gotten thirty, forty million children insured; we've still got ten who aren't, disproportionally black. And it's in the process of being destroyed unless we wake up. When I look at things going on in schools and kids going backwards, and the dropout rates among young black kids who are headed straight for child welfare, I mean I want to just stand up like Paul Revere and say, 'Stop! And, black community, wake up! Everybody, wake up!' So yes, I'm frustrated. We cannot let this happen on our watch."

One thing that gets me, that I've said many times on television, is when you see black people on television complain about affirmative

action or unfair treatment or racism in general, it's always some rich black person. Guys making $15 million a year.

"People like you and people like me who were prepared, we walk through the door," agreed Marian. "And we, in the black middle class, and the folks who got rich and the billionaires, we took advantage of all that opportunity. The folks who didn't have our parents and didn't have health care, who didn't have parents who had books in the house, they weren't prepared to walk through the door. It must be said that the best affirmative action programs are those that invest in children. A disproportionate number of black children start off way behind, without prenatal care, born with low birth weights, into families that are poor, where they don't have books in the house. What we have to do is to make sure that every child who is born has a level playing field. They should be *more* likely to get a preschool education, even though their parents have less to give them. Instead, they go to schools where they have the least experienced teachers, the most violence, whereas they ought to have the most experienced teachers, the best libraries. At every stage of their existence, the majority of black children were poor or have a totally unlevel playing field. And then you have your zero tolerance policies kick in, so an eight-year-old in Pittsburgh comes to school with a little scissors, and she's going to have an arrest on her record, when it should have been dealt with by the preacher or the principal.

"When crack came in, it just decimated our community, because it struck at the black mother who had always stood in the breach when everything was falling apart. The foster care system that we've begun to make progress on to get kids out is now absolutely overloaded. And so these kids are really going through life with every odd stacked against them. If they're lucky, a school counselor, a grandma, a somebody will grab one or two. I can tell you the most inspiring stories in the world, but we're losing, and if we don't stop this trend, we're going to be headed back to slavery. We've all got to wake up and reclaim our children and rebuild the bridge between the black middle class, the black wealthy, and the black poor, or the implications are just unthinkable. Our country's the only country in the industrialized world that doesn't provide health care for every child, that doesn't provide a good public education, that doesn't have after-school programs. We're not a child-friendly country, and we've got to build a movement for our children.

"It's complicated, and some of it's mixed up with race and the missions of worthy poor people. But we have never, unlike most of the countries of Europe or of Canada, said that children are not responsible for the lottery of their birth. And regardless of what parents may or may not be able to do, and I do believe that parents are the most responsible, we're going to make sure either because it makes economic sense or because it's morally right not to punish a two-year-old for the chance of his parents, that this child is provided with the basic means of survival. I think that should be the birthright of any child in the richest nation on earth.

"We have the highest child poverty rate in the industrialized world. No other country has one of five of its children poor, and among black children it's close to one in three, okay? The only thing this country will guarantee every child is a prison or detention cell after they get into trouble. It's the stupidest investment policy: They spend an average three times more for prison than for public school. We believe that prevention is a whole lot cheaper than prison, just as preventive health care costs a whole lot less than emergency care. I never dreamed it would be so hard to get our country to do for its children what it should be doing."

Everything Marian was saying sounded like common sense to me, just good common sense. So I asked her why the message isn't getting through.

"The message is not getting through for a bunch of reasons," she said. "Look back to how change finally came about in the civil rights movement. We had three networks in the fifties and the sixties when the civil rights movement started, and they all showed the same pictures of the dogs and the fire hoses and the children, and their issues were very clean and clear. We also had a group of civil rights supporters in *The New York Times* and *The Washington Post* who knew the context of all of these issues and did serious reporting of civil rights. Plus, we had charismatic leaders, we had great legal minds like Charles Houston and Thurgood Marshall, and we had great drama that attracted attention. And look how children and young people stepped up to the plate. I look back at the time that Dr. King and Dr. Mays and Whitney Young all were stepping up, and they were nurturing the young folks and giving them outlets for their frustration even as they were often following the young people. But the youth also had enough adults in our lives that we could do this thing together.

"We've got to have that kind of movement again. This is why we've been feeding new black leadership. You have to have a kind of readiness and leadership training to prepare people for a movement and give them skills. That's what we've been doing, over the last ten years, quietly, quietly preparing, 'cause we know it's going to come.

"A major challenge is that today you can't get anything but a ten-second message out, so how do you deal with the complexities of the issues? These issues are complex. It's about the substance of civil rights, it's about the quality of education; it's not pure discrimination, it's about when the government is going to dismantle fifty years of progress in a budget resolution that's in a language that most people don't know how to speak. You cannot get through the media when there are one hundred channels, and a lot of those are entertainment and hip-hop. It's the fragmentation of media. It's just so hard to get a message out to national media, 'cause it's controlled in large part by whoever's powerful, by political powers. We're back down trying to go to local papers, back to some of the old ways of A. Philip Randolph. We've got to go back to go underneath the national media to begin to get our complex, dangerous story out. Also, good news is not news in today's media. You know, when people were killing people in Cabrini Green, that was on the front page. With the overre-porting of crime and bad news, it's very hard to get the positive out there. That's one of the things we're struggling with. How do you communicate the bad news of a revolution that's going to undo all of our children's programs? It's hard."

Since I was born in Alabama at the time of the Birmingham church bombings, I was forced, in a sense, to follow the civil rights movement. So I understand. Plus, my mother and my grandmother raised me with the attitude of "Hey, you need to know this." I asked Marian if

she thought the majority of young black kids in schools today are learning anything about their history and the civil rights movement. She said no.

"We have been trying to get as many of the elders to come back and tell college students and high school students what children did, what adults did. Also, we're getting adults on tape before they die, and we've been doing that for ten, twelve years so they can see it. We have had the most extraordinary meetings with people of six generations from the young to the old folks who were there, and the children say, 'Why didn't you tell us? I mean, I'm sitting out here in a suburban area, I'm not called nigger or I'm not shot at or picked up as a black male on the streets. I don't care how middle class I am: Why didn't you tell us, why didn't you prepare us?' And what's our answer? Because we thought we had fixed it for you. These kids want to know but they don't know. We've let them down. They don't know their history."

I've seen that with my daughter, who's now fifteen. I was trying to explain to her about Dr. King one day. In Alabama you're taught that he was a black guy who wanted equal rights and he got assassinated. That's pretty much all you're taught as far as civil rights. It's very rare that they mention Medgar Evers; they definitely go out of their way not to mention Malcolm X. But that's pretty much the extent of what most people are taught in black history or American history in most schools. They don't have any idea what it was really like.

Marian agreed. "We've got to teach our kids every way we know how," she said. "The Jewish have their preschools, their Saturday schools. We've got to do it in our Freedom Schools, we've got to do it in our churches. When I was growing up, I lived in segregated times, but we had oratorical contests every eleventh grade, and I still remember my oration on how barriers of race can be surmounted. We need to have oratorical contests in churches, in mosques. We had some great black leaders come through. We learned who we were, how to dress, how to hold the door open, how to say thank you and ma'am, how to relate to folks, how to succeed. I mean, we worked hard, but you don't get that anywhere else. You can say that they're supposed to learn it at home, but they don't."

For most people, if you have a mom and dad, there's a really good chance you're going to get it. But, unfortunately, and I think this is the worst thing, the black family got killed by single-parent homes. I was with Tony Kornheiser and Mike Wilbon talking about this one night, and Mike asked Tony, "When you have a jackass in the Jewish neighborhood, what do y'all do?" Tony said, "We get rid of him." Now, I grew up in a small rural town in Alabama, and we all knew who served and sold drugs, we all knew who had ten kids and no job, so why is it that we don't hold each other more accountable? Why do we accept kids selling drugs in our neighborhoods, things like that?

"Well, we ought not to," Marian said. "We need to be running them out, and we need to be providing other work for the kids and the drug dealers. In my daddy's time, my church was open all the time and he had boxing in the church. When the parents can't function, the churches have got to function, the neighborhood has to function; everybody was in the church, and you know, we owned the children. And in that time, we ran out the people who were threatening folk and we all knew what was clearly right and wrong. If I'm in my hometown now, someone like my daddy doesn't exist. But there's a man named Reverend Love, an AME [African Methodist Episcopal] minister who runs Freedom Schools, and he's gotten an AME church to go and adopt a class. They've got substance programs, and they are the parents and the support for the parents who can't support themselves. You need five or six people in a town who stand up and say, here is what's right, here is what's good, here are the things we're going to fight for you to have in your schools and in your programs."

This conversation with Marian confirmed again for me how important this subject is. And I'm frustrated because I'm really concerned about these young black kids. I feel there's been a gradual decline and it's getting worse, not better.

One thing I just don't understand is how we got away from thinking education is a good thing. Because in this country that's the only way you're going to make it. Okay, if you can get forty points a game, a bunch of rebounds, you're going to make it, they're going to find you. But the truth of the matter is that most people have to make it academically. Why is it that black kids criticize those who do well? Why would they say you're trying to be white if you're trying to be smart or you're trying to do the right thing? How can it be that if you do bad stuff, that makes you more black? The phrase kids use now is _street cred_. For some reason our culture says, "Oh, you're trying to be white." How can we change our mindset not to think that we're inferior, to beat ourselves down all the time? That's what I'm looking for.

But if I was saddened by much of what Edelman and others told

me, I was also encouraged by the ways so many are trying to help. And I keep reminding myself of the words she left me with: "If you can go and highlight some of these problems, you can reach these young people in ways that I and many others cannot," she said. "You can say there's hope, and if there are people fighting for you, there's another way."

I feel that this book is the most important thing I've ever done.

AFTERWORD

There are a hundred lessons I learned or had reinforced during the conversations you've just read, whether from a former president of the United States or from Ice Cube, who went from simply enduring the conditions he grew up in around Compton, California, to making mainstream movies that are frequently the number one box-office attractions in America.

Probably the most important thing I'll take away from this project is that a lot of successful people truly welcome the opportunity to talk about race. The problem is that nobody asks them. I think people who are secure in their accomplishments aren't afraid of the topic at all. I was reminded that talent has no color.

That's why sports and entertainment, at the highest levels of performance, are almost colorproof. And they're unique in America because of that. If you live in Philadelphia and you don't know any black people or tend to be wary of black people, you were sure as hell loving Donovan McNabb in January 2005. When I was playing for the Phoenix Suns, a lot of people in Arizona hadn't previously come into contact with any black people. But when we went to the NBA finals in 1993, suddenly the whole state seemed to embrace our team in a way that transcended simply rooting for a basketball team.

There are so few places where people of different colors interact that folks who are celebrities, black or white, and folks who have had a wide range of experiences have had to take the lead. The people we talked to for this book were, it seems to me, secure people, which is probably why they said yes in the first place when I asked them to talk on the record about something that's fairly controversial.

But these conversations reminded me that prejudice is learned behavior. Actually, it's taught behavior. You're not born with those urges. I really believe people want to do better. They want to get along. In a lot of cases, they don't know how and they're afraid. But they're willing to give it a shot. They're willing to see Samuel L. Jackson in a movie regardless of him being a black man if they think the movie is good. What I'm trying to get across, as a final thought, is that if you encourage people to venture beyond their natural environment and get them to interact with people they believe are different, they'll find that we have a lot more in common than we think. But silence isn't going to get it done. Ignoring the problem isn't going to get it done. Clinging to old stereotypes isn't going to get it done. Dialogue is the best place to start. Hell, it's the only place to start.